The Storytime Sourcebook

A Compendium of Ideas and Resources for Storytellers

By

Carolyn N. Cullum

Neal-Schuman Publishers

New York   London

Published by Neal-Schuman Publishers, Inc.
23 Leonard Street
New York, NY 10013

Printed and bound in the United States of America

Library of Congress Cataloging-in-Publication Data

Cullum, Carolyn N.
   The storytime sourcebook : a compendium of ideas and resources for storytellers / Carolyn N. Cullum
   p.   cm.
   Includes bibliographical references and indexes.
   ISBN 1-55570-067-5
   1. Storytelling.   2. Libraries, Children's—Activity programs.
I.   Title.
Z718.3.C85   1990
027.61'51--dc20
                                                                90-49657
                                                                    CIP

Contents

Preface

Stories and storytelling existed long before the printed page. Children and adults alike would gather before the storytellers to hear tales of fancy, myth, or history. With the revival of storytelling in the United States, children's librarians have held regular storyhour programs in their local libraries.

The planning and execution of these story programs for preschool children takes a great deal of the children's librarian's time. For the past eleven years, I have served as a children's librarian for both school and public libraries. With a background in elementary education, educational media, and library science, I have prepared myself to deal with the task of introducing children to the immense amount of literature available to them.

For years I have prepared and executed a great many storyhours in many forms (books, flannel stories, films, poems, etc.), but unfortunately, none of these prepared programs were ever kept on file for future use. In order to assist others who wish to present similar programs, I've compiled this comprehensive subject guide to storyhour sessions. I have reconstructed and added to my original research. Many librarians will be at least partially relieved of the endless hours of research time needed to coordinate activities with stories for their future storyhour programs by availing themselves of this material. The aim of *Storytime Sourcebook* is to be a reference book to help you locate the appropriate idea (craft, fingerplay, story, song, etc.) needed for your program or lesson from the vast number of wonderful books already available in public libraries.

The activities and stories in this guide have been selected for use by librarians, teachers, media specialists, and others who work with children three to seven years old.

Storytime Sourcebook includes 446 picture books (broadly interpreted here to include fiction and nonfiction with a vocabulary level from preschool to second grade), 351 filmstrips, 93 16mm films and 156 videocassettes, all with full bibliographic citations to the publishers on 100 different topics chosen in order to:

- widen the children's experience with literature
- formulate programs related to the physical, emotional, and intellectual concerns of the child and
- encourage the sharing of experiences with other children of the same age.

Through storytelling children can learn about themselves and the world around them. I hope *Storytime Soucebook* will make the task of the storyhour leader a little easier.

How to Use This Book

Arrangement

Book titles, filmstrips, films, and videocassettes were selected from searches of actual library collections, published reviews and media catalogs. Except for videos, all material is arranged in alphabetical order by the subject chosen for each session. Those using video as an alternative to filmstrips and 16mm may check for the identical titles (where available) in the guide to 3/4"-videocassettes in Appendix B.

Each page represents one storyhour session on a single subject area of interest to children. By obtaining the books listed on your selected page and topic you will have complete directions for your activities. Included under each topic are:

Filmstrips or Films

Four or five filmstrips or 16mm film on each subject are listed with citations to the publisher, cost, and length.

Books

Picture books (fiction and nonfiction) related to each topic are listed. The prices indicated in the bibliography are the most recent available for each book.

Although not all the books listed will be in print (children's books go in and out of print quickly), you should be able to find most of them in your local library.

If your local library does not own the book you want, ask the children's librarian to ILL (Inter-Library Loan) the book from a neighboring library. Many public libraries are equipped to offer this service which locates a book from public libraries throughout the state within a week or two. This service is usually free and will save you time searching from place to place.

Fingerplays

These include short rhyming stories or poems that are very useful for filling in during transition times between activities. Using fingerplay with children helps them develop their fine motor skills by moving their fingers to act out the rhyme, increases their vocabulary, teaches them new concepts, or may just help them relax after a particularly active game.

Many parents have done simple fingerplay games with their child already by introducing "This Little Piggie" or "Pat-A-Cake." You can expand on these by using the fingerplays suggested on each page. The source for the fingerplay will give you the actual verse along with suggested finger motions to mimic the words.

When teaching a fingerplay to a young child be sure to do the following:

- Begin by teaching the motions alone without the verse.

- Mirror the motions when you are facing the group. If you want the group to wave their right hand—*you* wave the left, etc.

- Add the verse once the motions have become familiar and allow plenty of opportunity for repetition.

- Enjoy it yourself. If you aren't having fun, neither will the children.

Crafts

Simple, easy to assemble crafts related to the topic are described briefly on each page. Sources for craft ideas are cited, unless they are original. For complete instructions on the craft, you would have to procure the source-book. All the crafts suggested use inexpensive materials and do not require skill in art.

Activity

Physical activities of some kind are essential during an hour-long program with preschool children. Attention spans differ and by alternating active and passive periods the leader keeps the children's interest and control of the group.

A description of the games is related to the topic featured on each page. The original source of the game is stated if further clarification is needed.

Fingerplays and games listed on each page will give you active periods necessary to relieve the children's pent-up energies when their attention wanes.

Songs

Song titles are listed with a source for the music and lyrics.

Children enjoy singing and will ask for their favorite song for many days after they learn it. If they ask to repeat a song from a previous session, sing it then move on to a new one.

Don't be afraid to sing. Young children do not expect a trained voice, and in fact, a little mistake once in a while will only endear you to them.

Storytime Sourcebook also includes:

- Table of Contents (Subject Guide)
- Filmstrip Guide
- 16mm Film Index
- Videocassette Index (Includes those videos currently available as an alternative AV form to using filmstrips or 16mm film of the same title)
- Book Index (Both Title and Author)
- Craft Index
- Activities Index
- Song Index
- Book Publishers Index
- Film, Filmstrip, and Videocassette Distributors Index

An' all us other children, when the supper
      things is done,
We set around the kitchen fire an' has
      the mostest fun
A-list'ning' to the witch tales 'at Annie
      tells about
An' the gobble-uns 'at gits you
      Ef you
         Don't
            Watch
            Out!

James Whitcomb Riley
Little Orphan Annie

When we meet next we'll have a tale to tell.

Lord Byron
Don Juan

1 Activities: Reading

Filmstrips: *Arthur's Prize Reader*, EBEC
I Can Read with My Eyes Shut, Random House
Petunia, Weston Woods
When Will I Read?, Random House, Educational
Enrichment Materials

Books: *Too Many Books!*, Caroline Bauer
Johnny Lion's Book, Edith Hurd
The Once-Upon-a-Time Dragon, Jack Kent
Olaf Reads, Joan Lexau
That's Enough for One Day!, Susan Pearson

Fingerplay: Learning. (Source: *Resource Book for the Kindergarten Teacher*, Virginia H. Lucus and Walter B. Barbe)

Craft: "Touch-Me Books". Many children get their early experience with reading by using books that allow them to touch various textures included in the story. Try making your own "Touch-Me" book. Prepare a small three-page book with one large illustration and word per page. (Suggestion: Use a duck, a rabbit and a cat.)

At the program allow time to color the illustrations, then provide the appropriate textures to glue to the pictures (feathers, cottonballs (rabbit's tail), and pieces of fur). Children have a feeling of accomplishment by creating a book of their own for identifying textures as well as animals.

Activity: Word Matching. Using large flashcards with simple words (cat, ball, etc.) and illustrations on them, discuss the pictures and words with the children. Next pass out cards with only the words on them, and see how many children can match these to the flashcards.

The level of the words will depend on the age level of your group.

2 Alphabet

Filmstrips: *Alligators All Around,* Weston Woods
Curious George Learns the Alphabet, Random House
Hooper Humperdink..? Not Him!, Random House
Little Monster's Alphabet Book, Listening Library
A Merry Mouse Christmas A-B-C, SVE

Film: *The Shout It Out Alphabet Film,* Phoenix

Books: *C Is for Circus,* Bernice Chardiet
I Unpacked My Grandmother's Trunk, Susan Hoguet
Harold's ABC, Crockett Johnson
Pooh's Alphabet Book, A.A. Milne
The Sesame Street ABC Storybook, Jeffrey Moss

Fingerplay: ABC Fingers.   (Source: *Rhymes for Learning Times,* Louise Binder Scott)

Craft: Pick-a-Letter. Display all the letters of the alphabet somewhere in the room. Some children may know them all while others may recognize only a few. Have each child choose one letter that he or she knows and tell the group what it is. Next have each child take construction paper and in one corner draw a picture of something beginning with the letter. In the other corner trace the letter with glue and sprinkle with glitter. Design a cover for the new booklet, "My Alphabet Book," to which the child can add letters later as he or she learns them

Activity: The Manual Alphabet. Children are fascinated with the plight of the handicapped. When doing this program discuss the problems of a mute child communicating with his friends. Introduce a new type of alphabet, the manual alphabet. Although it would be too difficult and time-consuming to teach the entire alphabet at this age, trying teaching one or two key letters that the children choose themselves.   (Source: *Do a Zoom-Do,* Bernice Chesler)

Song: "The Alphabet Song" (Source: *The Reader's Digest Children's Songbook,* William L. Simon)

3 Anatomy: Body Parts

Filmstrips: *The Ear Book*, Random House
The Eye Book, Random House
Funny Feet, Random House, Educational Enrichment
Materials
Hand, Hand, Fingers, Thumb, Random House
The Nose Book, Random House

Books: *I'm Too Small, You're Too Big*, Judith Barret
The Me I See, Barbara Hazen
The Littlest Leaguer, Sydney Hoff
Happy Birthday, Sam, Patricia Hutchins
Eyes, Nose, Fingers, Toes, Ruth Krauss
Make a Face, Lynn Yudell

Fingerplay: Where is Thumbkin? (Source: *Eye Winker, Tom Tinker, Chin Chopper*, Tom Glazer)

Craft: Me-Doll. Everyone is unique in his or her own way but we also have many similarities, such as where our joints are located. Make a jointed "Me-Doll" just like yourself to show the children where the parts of the body bend. An easy and inexpensive method of construction is the use of paper and brass paper fasteners, among other items listed in the source below. Have the children make their own "Me-Doll" after seeing themselves in a full-length mirror, then compare how we are each very special. (Source: *Purple Cow to the Rescue*, Ann Cole, Carolyn Haas, and Betty Weinberger)

Activity and Song: "Who Has a Nose?". Done to the tune of Frére Jacques, this song and activity cover the range of body parts familiar to children including the concept of short and tall. Even the shyest child will participate in a group and with a song that repeats its verses. Additional verses might even be suggested by the children themselves. (Source: *Dancing Games for Children of all Ages*, Esther L. Nelson)

4 Animals

Filmstrips:	*The Camel with the Wrinkled Knees*, SVE
	Henny Penny, Coronet
	Little Fox Goes to the End of the World, Imperial
	    Educational Resources
	There's a Hippopotamus Under My Bed, Random
	    House, Educational Enrichment Materials
	The Three Little Pigs, Weston Woods

Film:	*The Camel Who Took a Walk*, Weston Woods
Books:	*Animals Should Definitely Not Wear Clothing*, Judi Barrett *A Bargain for Frances*, Russell Hoban *Sammy the Seal*, Syd Hoff *Katy No-Pocket*, Emmy Payne *Sylvester and the Magic Pebble*, William Steig

Fingerplay: Seals. (Source: *Finger Frolics—Revised*, Liz Cromwell, Dixie Hibner, and John R. Faitel)

Craft: Panda Puppet. Hand puppets are always a sure favorite with this age level. Precut pieces or patterns are advisable in large groups. Felt is an easy material to work with. Try constructing a held panda puppet. Though the source indicated below suggests sewing the edges, a fast-drying material glue (Slomon's Velverette Craft Glue or similar types found in craft stores) would be sufficient to hold the puppet together. A box stage can be used to practice with the new creation. (Source: *Felt Craft*, Florence Temko)

Activity: Fox and Rabbits: Divide the players into two teams, the "Foxes" and the "Rabbits." At one end of the room mark an area representing home for the rabbits. Throughout the room designate a few small circles as safe rabbit holes. The rabbits try to get safely from one end of the room to home while the foxes try to tag them. Have the teams change roles and play again. The team with the fewest eliminated wins. (Source: *500 Games*, Peter L. Cave)

Song:	"Old MacDonald" (Source: *Eye Winker, Tom Tinker, Chin Chopper*, Tom Glazer)

5 Animals: Bears

Filmstrips: *The Bear Detectives*, Random House
Big Bear to the Rescue, EBEC
A Kiss for Little Bear, Weston Woods
Paddington Helps Out: Paddington Dines Out,
    Learning Tree Filmstrips
Winnie the Pooh and Tigger, Too!, Walt Disney
    Educational Media

Films: *The Bear and the Fly*, Weston Woods
Blueberries for Sal, Weston Woods

Books: *Moon Bear*, Frank Asch
Ask Mr. Bear, Marjorie Flack
Good Morning, Baby Bear, Eric Hill
The Three Bears, Margaret Hillert
Blueberries for Sal, Robert McCloskey

Fingerplay: This Little Bear. (Source: *Finger Frolics—Revised*, Liz Cromwell, Dixie Hibner, and John R. Faitel)

Craft: Teddy Bear—Fuzzy Friend: Let's make a teddy bear character with a soft, furry texture. Begin by cutting a basic bear form from cardboard or poster board. Add decorative texture by cutting short lengths of brown yarn and gluing it to the bear form. Finish your fuzzy friend by adding nose, eyes, and the pads of the paws with construction paper or felt. (Source: *The Fun-To-Make Book*, Colette Lamargue)

Activity: The Bear Is in His Cave. Show a group of children a selection of objects on the floor. Have them turn their backs and recite a given verse (see the source listed below). While the others are reciting have another child pretend to be a bear creeping in to carry away one object. The first child to identify the missing object will now become the bear.

This game can be played with any number of children and objects. It can also be adjusted to help you introduce specific items to the children, such as, the four food groups, animals, toys, or toy trucks for things that go. (Source: *New Games to Play*, Juel Krisvoy)

Song: "The Bear Went Over the Mountain" (Source: *The Fireside Book of Birds and Beasts*, Jane Yolen)

6 Animals: Cats

Filmstrips: *Adventures of a Kitten*, Imperial Film Co.
The Cat in the Hat, Random House
Harry the Hider, Imperial Film Co.
The Shy Little Kitten, Random House, Miller-Brody

Films: *Millions of Cats*, Weston Woods
Owl and the Pussycat, Weston Woods

Books: *Have You Seen My Cat?*, Eric Carle
Millions of Cats, Wanda Gag
Kitten for a Day, Ezra Keats
The Fat Cat, Jack Kent
Orange Oliver, Robert Lasson

Fingerplay: A Kitten. (Source: *Finger Frolics—Revised*, Liz Cromwell, Dixie Hibner, and John R. Faitel)

Craft: Egg Carton Pussycat: Egg cartons can be transformed into different objects of art. Using this simple, easily obtainable material the children can make a black cat by cutting, painting, and mounting the ears, eyes, and mouth with paper. Try pipe cleaners for whiskers. Other simple characters are also suggested and illustrated in the source listed below. (Source: *Instructor's Artfully Easy!*, no author)

Activity: Cat and Rat. This game can be played by any number of players over six-years-old. One child, acting as the rat, stands in the center of a circle formed by the other children. Another player, the cat, attempts to break through the circle to tag the rat. If he does so, the rat is allowed to choose someone else to be the rat and he becomes the cat.

This can be continued as long as desired. It can be used as a fill-in activity when other activities suddenly finish earlier than expected. Another plus is that there are no real losers. (Source: *Games*, Anne Rockwell)

Song: "Three Little Kittens" (Source: *The Fireside Songbook of Birds and Beasts*, Jane Yolen)

7 Animals: Dogs

Filmstrips: *No Roses for Harry*, Random House, Miller-Brody
The Pokey Little Puppy, Random House,
    Miller-Brody
Pluto's Fledgling, Walt Disney Educational Media
Pretzel, Random House Educational Enrichment
    Materials
Raggedy Ann and Fido, SVE

Films: *Angus Lost*, Phoenix
A Boy, a Dog, and a Frog, Phoenix
Madeline's Rescue, Rembrandt Films

Books: *Madeline's Rescue*, Ludwig Bemelmans
Clifford's Good Deeds, Norman Bridwell
Claude and Pepper, Dick Gackenbach
Whistle for Willie, Ezra J. Keats
Harry the Dirty Dog, Gene Zion

Craft: Paper Bag Dog: Paper-bag creations are one of the easiest and least expensive of crafts. They are also great fun for children. Try making a paper-bag dog mask. Use a brown grocery bag, and cut a hole on one side the size of the child's face.

Discuss with the children the parts of a dog's face. You can use construction paper to put long, floppy ears on the side. Get some clown make-up to color the child's nose black.

Activity: My Little Dog. This game is similar to the well-known "Duck, Duck, Goose." This can be played with any number of children in a circle or on opposite ends of the room. Designate a section of the room to be the dog's home. With most of the children at one end of the room and two children (the dog and his master) at the home base the game can begin. The master walks his dog from the home, down the street past the other children while reciting the verse (text in source listed below) asking someone to take care of his dog. When the master names another player, the new player chases the dog around the room hoping to tag him before he gets home. The new player now can be the new dog. (Source: *New Games to Play*, Juel Krisvoy)

Song: "Bingo" (Source: *The Reader's Digest Children's Songbook*, William L. Simon)

8 Animals: Elephants

Filmstrips: *Dumbo*, Walt Disney Educational Media
Horton Hatches an Egg, Random House
Meet Babar and His Family, Random House
The Saggy Baggy Elephant, Random House,
Miller-Brody
Where Can an Elephant Hide?, Spoken Arts

Films: *Circus Baby*, Weston Woods
The Elephant's Child, Coronet

Books: *Oliver*, Syd Hoff
The Ant and the Elephant, Bill Peet
The Circus Baby, Maud Petersham
Alistair's Elephant, Marilyn Sadler
Smallest Elephant in the World, Alvin Tresselt

Fingerplay: Five Gray Elephants. (Source: *Finger Frolics—Revised*, Liz Cromwell, Dixie Hibner, and John R. Faitel)

Craft: A Paper Bag Elephant. Your own toy elephant can be formed by stuffing a lunch bag with tissue and tying off one end. Twist the end tied off again to form the nose. Eyes and ears may be made with construction paper or paint. Braid yarn for the elephant's tail and simple clip clothespins are ideal for legs. (Source: *Simply Fun! Things to Make and Do*, James Razzi)

Activity: Zoo Hunt. Zoo animals are familiar to most children. This simple game of charades allows the children to pretend they are various animals as well as trying to guess what animals others are portraying. Write down the names of familiar zoo animals, and distribute them among the group so they know which animal they will pretend to be.

If, as in most storyhour programs, your children are non-readers use simple animal flashcards with illustrations. Avoid breaking the group into teams which would end in someone losing. (Source: *500 Games*, Peter L. Cave)

Song: "One Elephant Went Out to Play" (Source: *Dancing Games for Children of All Ages*, Esther L. Nelson)

9 Animals: Lions and Tigers

Filmstrips: *Andy and the Lion*, Weston Woods
    Dandelion, Live Oak Media
    The Happy Lion's Treasure, EBEC
    Lambert, The Sheepish Lion, Random House, Miller-
        Brody
    Tawny Scrawny Lion, Random House, Miller-Brody

Films: *Leo on Vacation*, Phoenix
    The Lion and the Mouse, Coronet

Books: *The Lion and the Mouse*, Aesop
    The Sleepy Little Lion, Margaret Brown
    The Happy Lion, Louise Fatio
    The Terrible Tiger, Jack Prelutsky
    The Tiger Hunt, Mady Villarejo

Fingerplay: Tiger Walk. (Source: *Rhymes for Learning Times*, Louise Binder Scott)

Craft: Lion Face. Using a paper plate, have the children draw the eyes, nose, and mouth of a lion with markers. Cut strips of yellow construction paper to be glued all the way around the perimeter of the plate to form the lion's mane. You may curl each strip using scissors.

If you would care to turn this into a mask you can simply add string to the sides or better yet put it on a stick to be held in the child's hand.

Activity: Lions and Tigers. Divide the room with tape or string. One player is chosen to be a tiger and one chosen to be the lion, each on opposite ends of the room. Other players may move anywhere they want while the tiger and lion may not cross into the other's den.

Any players the lion or tiger can tag must remain in their den. The animal that catches the most victims will win. (Source: *500 Games*, Peter L. Cave)

Song: "The Zoo" (Source: *Music for Ones and Twos*, Tom Glazer)

10 Animals: Mice

Filmstrips: *Alexander and the Wind-up Mouse*, Random House
Anatole, EBEC
Frederick, Random House
How Not to Catch a Mouse, BFA Educational Media
Mickey Mouse, The Brave Little Tailor, Walt Disney
    Educational Media

Films: *Anatole and the Piano*, McGraw
Norman the Doorman, Weston Woods

Books: *Do You Want to be My Friend?*, Eric Carle
Max the Mouse, James Cressey
The Perfect Mouse, Dick Gackenbach
Geraldine, the Music Mouse, Leo Lionni
The Story of Jumping Mouse, John Steptoe

Fingerplay: Hickory Dickory Dock. (Source: *Finger Frolics—Revised*, Liz Cromwell, Dixie Hibner, and John R. Faitel)

Craft: Mousie Paperweight. The "Pet Rock" craze has allowed us all to have our own little pets by using stones or rocks from our own backyard. To make your own mousie paperweight or pet mouse use a smooth round stone for the basic body. The tail can be added by cutting a small piece of curled wire such as found in a spiral notebook. Cut eyes, ears, nose, and mouth from felt; whiskers can be made from broomstick straw or pipe cleaners. (Source: *Instructor's Artfully Easy!*, no author)

Activity: Three Blind Mice. "Three Blind Mice" is a familiar song to children at this age and will create a comfortable foundation for the following game:
    The children form a circle with one in the center (farmer's wife). As they dance around singing and run for the nearest wall, the farmer's wife tries to catch one person (mouse) who will become the next farmer's wife. (Source: *500 Games*, Peter L. Cave)

Song: "Three Blind Mice" (Source: *Sing Hey Diddle Diddle*, Beatrice Harrop)

11   Animals: Monkeys

Filmstrips: *Arthur's Honey Bear,* EBEC
Arthur's Pen Pal, EBEC
Cecily G. and the Nine Monkeys, Random House,
     Educational Enrichment Materials
Curious George, Random House, Educational Enrichment
     Materials
Hand, Hand, Fingers, Thumb, Random House

Film: *Caps for Sale,* Weston Woods

Books: *Last One Home Is a Green Pig,* Edith Hurd
Run, Little Monkeys, Run, Run, Run, Charles Kepes
The Monkey That Went to School, Leonard Meshover
     and Sally Feistel
Curious George Flies a Kite, Margaret Rey
Caps for Sale, Esphyr Slobodkina

Fingerplay: Two Little Monkeys. (Source: *Finger Frolics—Revised,* Liz
Cromwell, Dixie Hibner, and John R. Faitel)

Craft: Silly Salt-Box Monkey. A salt box can be made into a container for
collecting prize possessions. With the youngest children you may wish to
have parts precut for this craft. This may be made into a monkey with the
use of construction paper and glue. Begin with a collection of salt box
animals. (Source: *Sticks and Stones and Ice Cream Cones,* Phyllis Fiarotta)

Activity: Monkey See, Monkey Do.

> Monkey see, Monkey do
> I can _____ and you can, too.

Play this game in the same method as Simon Says substituting the word
'monkey' for Simon.

Song: "Pop! Goes the Weasel" (Source: *The Golden Song Book,*
Katharine Tyler Wessells)

12 Animals: Rabbits

Filmstrips: *The Happy Lion's Rabbits,* EBEC
Hunches in Bunches, Random House
Two Hundred Rabbits, Live Oak Media
Little Rabbit's Loose Tooth, Pied Piper Productions
The Tortoise and the Hare, Walt Disney Educational
    Media

Film: *Morris' Disappearing Bag,* Weston Woods

Books: *Hattie Be Quiet, Hattie Be Good,* Dick Gackenbach
Carrot Cake, Nonny Hogrogian
The Habits of Rabbits, Virginia Kahl
The Hunt for Rabbit's Galosh, Ann Schweninger
Mr. Rabbit and the Lovely Present, Charlotte Zolotow

Fingerplay: A Bunny. (Source: *Finger Frolics—Revised,* Liz Cromwell, Dixie Hibner, and John R. Faitel)

Craft: Silly Salt-Box Bunny. A salt box can be made into a container for collecting prize possessions. With the youngest children you may wish to have parts precut for this craft. This may be made into a bunny with the use of construction paper and glue. Begin with a collection of salt box animals.

If you are using this for an Easter program, you may wish to treat the children to an Easter surprise by filling it with paper grass and a special treat. (Source: *Sticks and Stones and Ice Cream Cones,* Phyllis Fiarotta)

Activity: The Bunny Hop. This simple dance will allow the children to pretend to be bunnies while moving around the entire room. A good physical activity between nonactive stories. (Source: *The Reader's Digest Children's Songbook,* William L. Simon)

Song: "Little Rabbit Foo-Foo" (Source: *Do Your Ears Hang Low?,*
    Tom Glazer)

13 Art

Filmstrips: *Bear Hunt*, Weston Woods
Harold and the Purple Crayon, Weston Woods
The Magical Drawings of Mooney B. Finch, Listening
Library
Norman the Doorman, Weston Woods
A Picture for Harold's Room, Weston Woods

Books: *Bear Hunt*, Anthony Browne
Daniel's Duck, Clyde Bulla
Ernie's Little Lie, Dan Elliott
Emma, Wendy Kesselman
The Bear's Picture, Daniel Pinkwater

Fingerplay and Activity: Draw a Person in the Air. (Source: *Finger Frolics—Revised*, Liz Cromwell, Dixie Hibner, and John R. Faitel)

Craft: Potato or Ink Pad Printing. Children are fond of working with any type of printing materials. Try potato printing. With this can you can arrange any design by cutting it from a potato then using ink pads and paper to design cards, pictures, etc.

If time doesn't permit you to use potato printing, try collecting various styles of ink stamps and the children will do the rest. (Source: *The Fun-To-Make Book*, Colette Lamargue)

Activity: Color Hunt. Divide the children into small groups and designate a color for that team by hanging around each member's neck a string with a piece of colored paper attached to it.

Hide a number of objects in the room that are the same color as those selected for the groups. The number of objects selected will vary with your group sizes, but each group should have an equal number to look for.

At a given signal, allow all to hunt for the items that are the same color as their group. The first group to find them all and return them to their base wins. Repeat the game by changing group colors or mixing up the members of the groups again

14 Babies

Filmstrips: *A Baby Sister for Frances*, BFA Educational Media
The Box with the Red Wheels, MacMillan
Hush Little Baby, Weston Woods
Peter's Chair, Weston Woods

Film: *Smile for Auntie*, Weston Woods

Books: *Billy and Our New Baby*, Helen Arnstein
Starbaby, Frank Asch
Go and Hush the Baby, Betsy Byars
The Bravest Babysitter, Barbara Greenberg
Couldn't We Have a Turtle Instead?, Judith Vigna

Fingerplay: Baby. (Source: *Finger Frolics—Revised*, Liz Cromwell, Dixie Hibner, and John R. Faitel)

Craft: Baby Doll Beds. A small baby doll cradle can be constructed using an oatmeal box. When a portion is cut away and the box painted and decorated, it will make an ideal rocking cradle for small children to enjoy.

In case you don't want a cradle, a simple bunk bed can be made by using a shoe box.

Decorations for either bed can be made with paint (a material greatly enjoyed by children) and stickers. (Source: *Just a Box?*, Goldie Taub Chernoff)

Activity: Hush Little Baby. This old American lullaby is an easy piece to sing and act out with a small group. Nelson gives suggestions for different children acting out the parts of the mockingbird, billy goat, etc., as well as music for the song.

Once the children are familiar with the parts they are going to play, repeat the song as many times as the children desire. Games which allow the children to sing, and move about provide a good outlet for pent-up energies. (Source: *Dancing Games for Children of All Ages*, Esther L. Nelson)

Song: "John Brown's Baby" (Source: *The Silly Song-book*, Esther L. Nelson)

15 Bedtime Stories

Suggestion: Do this program at night and invite the children to wear their pajamas and bring their teddy bears.

Filmstrips: *Bedtime for Frances*, BFA Educational Media
Goodnight, Owl!, Weston Woods
Ira Sleeps Over, Live Oak Media
Mother, Mother, I Want Another, Imperial
Educational Resources
There's a Nightmare in My Closet, Listening Library

Film: *The Napping House*, Weston Woods

Books: *Goodnight, Moon*, Margaret Brown
Frances, Face-maker, William Cole
The Bed Book, Sylvia Plath
We Can't Sleep, James Stevenson
Goodnight Max, Hanne Turk

Fingerplay: Little Bear. (Source: *Finger Frolics—Revised*, Liz Cromwell, Dixie Hibner, and John R. Faitel)

Craft: Night's Nice. After discussing what happens at night and asking the children to identify what they see in the sky at night, pass out materials for the children to make their own night sky. This is simple enough for young children. A piece of black paper, one yellow sticker dot (moon) and star stickers are all that is needed for them to enjoy themselves.

Activity: Ten in a Bed. This simple song may be adapted to the size of the group by changing the number and beginning of countdown. It may be a simple fingerplay/song or can be acted out with the children. Tom Glazer's simple-to-follow directions, and sheet music for piano and guitar are provided in the source stated here. Many of his songs can be used with this age group. They are easy and lots of fun for both parents and children. (Source: *Do Your Ears Hang Low?*, Tom Glazer)

Song: "Twinkle, Twinkle Little Star" (Source: *The Golden Song Book*, Katharine Tyler Wessells)

16 Behavior: Losing Things

Filmstrips: *Andrew and the Strawberry Monsters,* EBEC
Babar Loses His Crown, Random House
Frog and Toad Are Friends: A Lost Button, Random
House, Miller-Brody
Three Little Kittens, Random House
Stop That Ball, Random House

Books: *Nu Dang and His Kite,* Jacqueline Ayer
The Blanket, John Burningham
Finders Keepers, Losers Weepers, Joan Lexau
The Trip, Marjorie Sharmat
Little Brown Bear Loses His Clothes, Elizabeth
Upham

Fingerplay: Little Bo-Peep. (Source: *Finger Frolics—Revised,* Liz Cromwell, Dixie Hibner, and John R. Faitel)

Craft: The Kitten's Mittens. Using various color construction paper, cut out enough mitten shapes to allow each child to have a matching pair. One method of getting the child more involved in the craft is to give each child only one mitten in the color of his choice. Place the matching mittens in the front of the room or hide them around the room, and allow the children to search for the match.

Now give the children crayons, glitter (if you don't mind the mess), and sticker dots and stars (an all-time favorite with toddlers). Allow them to decorate the mittens to their own taste. Finally, give them string to attach one to the other and hang their creations around their necks.

This can also be a nice decoration to hang on the library or classroom windows. (Source: *101 Easy Art Activities,* Trudy Aarons and Francine Koelsch)

Activity: Button, Button, Who's Got the Button? This game is for eight or more players. One player sits in the center of a circle formed by the other players. The players in the circle have a button they pass from hand to hand. They keep their hands moving so the center player thinks the button is still being passed and he must guess who has the button. (Source: *Games,* Anne Rockwell)

Song: "Three Little Kittens" (Source: *Singing-Bee!: A Collection of Favorite Children's Songs,* Jane Hart)

17 Behavior: Wishing

Filmstrips: *I Wish I Had Duck Feet*, Random House
Johnny's Birthday Wish, Clearvue
The Poor Woodcutter and the Dove, EBEC
Someday, Educational Enrichment Materials/
    Random House
The Story of King Midas, EBEC

Books: *Don't Ever Wish for a 7 Ft. Bear*, Robert Benton
Three Wishes, Lucille Clifton
The Wishing Hat, Annegert Fuchshuber
Jeanne-Marie Counts Her Sheep, Francoise Seignobosc
Someday, Said Mitchell, Barbara Williams

Fingerplay: Birthday Celebration. (Source: *Finger Frolics—Revised*, Liz Cromwell, Dixie Hibner, and John R. Faitel)

Craft: The Wishing Well. Use salt or oatmeal boxes to design a wishing well bank. Glue two popsicle sticks to the sides of the box to support a small tilted roof. Glue red paper to the exterior portion of the box, and have the children design the bricks with markers.

Use the newly made bank to save your money for other prizes you may be wishing for.

Activity: The Wishing Candle. Place a large candle in the center of a table. Each player should be blindfolded, then spun around three times near the table. The first who can blow out the wishing candle is the winner.

This activity can precede a discussion of what each child would wish for if he or she were granted one wish. (Caution: This game must be supervised by an adult.)

Songs: "When You Wish Upon a Star" (Source: *The Illustrated Disney Song Book*, David E. Tietyen)

18 Bicycles

Filmstrips: *The Bear's Bicycle,* Live Oak Media
Bicycle Safety: Safety on Wheels with Goofy,
    Walt Disney Educational Media
The Bike Lesson, Random House
I'm No Fool with a Bicycle, Walt Disney Educational
    Media
Winnie the Pooh on the Way to School: Rabbit Has a
    Bicycle Ride, Walt Disney Educational Media

Film: *Curious George Rides a Bike,* Weston Woods

Books: *The Groggs' Day Out,* Anne Bently
Shawn's Red Bike, Petronella Breinburg
The Bear's Bicycle, Emilie McLeod
Bicycle Bear, Michaela Muntean
Curious George Rides a Bike, Hans Rey

Fingerplay: My Little Tricycle. (Source: *Finger Frolics—Revised,* Liz Cromwell, Dixie Hibner, and John R. Faitel)

Activity: Bicycle Safety Course. With the cooperation of the local police department you might set up a small obstacle course for the children to ride their bicycles through. It should be emphasized to all that this is a safety course and not a race track.

You will need to close off a portion of your parking lot for this event and might even want to invite older children to attend. Chalk out a course to be followed by arrows. At various key spots in the course place a stop sign, a small ramp, and, if possible, a working traffic light.

Many police departments will send a police officer to speak with the children and will also donate such items as bike reflectors for those children completing the course.

Song: "The Doll and the Bike" (Source: *God's Wonderful World,*
    Agnes Leckie Mason and Phyllis Brown Ohanian)

19 Birds

Filmstrips: *Horton Hatches an Egg,* Random House
The Little Red Hen, Coronet
No One Noticed Ralph, Imperial Educational
  Resources
Petunia, Beware, Random House
The Ugly Duckling, Walt Disney Educational Media

Film: *Dorothy and the Ostrich,* Phoenix

Books: *Moon Bear,* Frank Asch
Penny Wise, Fun Foolish, Judy Delton
Hector Penguin, Louise Fatio
Quiet! There's a Canary in the Library, Don Freeman
Round Robin, Jack Kent

Fingerplay: Fly, Little Bird. (Source: *Rhymes for Learning Times,*
Louise Binder Scott)

Craft: Feed the Birds. Allow the children to make a bird feeder for their
backyard. Use a cardboard milk carton, and cut out two opposite sides to
allow birds to move through. Punch holes in the top section for yarn to tie
it to the tree. Decoration of the carton can be left to available materials.

Bird seed can be placed in the bottom of the feeder every other day.
(Source: *Lollipop, Grapes and Clothespin Critters: Quick, On-the-Spot Remedies
for Restless Children 2-10,* Robyn Freedman Spizman)

Activity: Humming Birds. This is a variation of "Hot and Cold." Have one
child turn his back while an object chosen is hidden somewhere in the room.
The reminder of the group watches where the object is hidden. As the first
child looks around the room to find the object the rest hums. The closer the
person gets to finding it the louder the humming will get, the further away
he gets the softer the children will hum.

This is a game that requires little preparation and can be played as long
as the interest is there. Another advantage here is that there are no winners
or losers. (Source: *500 Games,* Peter L. Cave)

Song: "Two Little Blackbirds" *The Fireside Book of Fun and Game
Songs,* Marie Winn

20 Birds: Ducks

Filmstrips: *Angus and the Ducks*, Weston Woods
Make Way for Ducklings, Weston Woods
Springtime for Jeanne-Marie, Random House, Miller-
    Brody
The Story About Ping, Weston Woods
The Ugly Duckling, Walt Disney Educational Media

Film: *Mother Duck and the Big Race*, Coronet

Books: *A Pet for Duck and Bear*, Judy Delton
Arnold of the Ducks, Mordicai Gerstein
Last One Home is a Green Pig, Edith Hurd
Howard, James Stevenson
Have You Seen My Duckling?, Nancy Tafuri

Fingerplay: Mr. Turkey and Mr. Duck. (Source: *Finger Frolics—Revised*, Liz Cromwell, Dixie Hibner, and John R. Faitel)

Craft: A Duck Friend. An illustration of a duck may be duplicated from the source indicated here. After each child has colored his duck, distribute feathers and glue so that the children can add a little texture to the illustration. If the picture has been reproduced on cardstock, it can then be cut out and mounted on a popsicle stick to create a stick puppet.

This craft activity is simple enough for even the two-year-old level. Their creations can be used to act out a duck story, (*Have You Seen My Duckling?* Nancy Tafuri) or to sing a song. (Source: *The Kids' Stuff Book of Patterns, Projects, and Plans*, Imogene Forte)

Activity: Duck, Duck, Goose. Have all the children (any number will work here) crouch in a circle in the center of the room. One child will walk around the perimeter of the circle saying, "Duck, Duck, Duck..." until he taps one child and says, "Goose." The 'goose' must get up and chase the child around the circle and tag him before he reaches the empty spot left in the circle. If he fails to reach the child in time he must go around the circle now.

For a variation of this game, try asking the children to waddle like a duck around the circle instead of running when trying to catch the goose.

Song: "The Little White Duck" (Source: *The Reader's Digest Children's Songbook*, Wiliam L. Simon)

21 Birds: Owls

Filmstrips: *Goodnight, Owl!*, Weston Woods
The Happy Owls, Weston Woods
The Owl and the Grasshopper, Random House
Sam and the Firefly, Random House

Film: *Owl and the Pussycat*, Weston Woods

Books: *Owliver*, Robert Kraus
Little Owl Leaves the Nest, Marcia Leonard
Owl at Home, Arnold Lobel
Wide-Awake Owl, Louis Slobodkin
The Owl and the Woodpecker, Brian Wildsmith

Fingerplay: Five Little Girls. (Source: *Rhymes for Learning Times*, Louise Binder Scott)

Craft: Owl Bank. A decorative owl bank will help the children to save their pennies for a rainy day. Use containers easily found in the home, such as, bread crumb containers or circular oatmeal boxes. Cover the container with a piece of burlap.

Contrasting colors of burlap can be used to make the eyes, beak, and feathers of the owl. If extra burlap isn't available try substituting colored construction paper. (Source: *Make it with Burlap*, Elyse Sommer)

Activity: Birds Can Fly. This game is a variation of the game "Simon Says." All players stand facing the child who is the leader. The leader begins the game by calling out "Birds can fly" and begins flapping his arms. Other players copy the leader's actions. The leader continues calling out with other flying animals (Butterflies can fly, etc.). At some point he can mention an animal that can't fly (Cows can fly). Any child still flapping his wings is out of the game. Continue until one child is left and that child is the next leader.

Other variations of this game can be continued with:
• Tigers can growl (everyone growls)
• Fish can swim (make swimming motions).
(Source: *500 Games*, Peter L. Cave)

Song: "Big Old Owl" (Source: *American Folk Songs for Children in Home, School and Nursery School*, Ruth Crawford Seeger)

22   Birds: Penguins

Filmstrips: *The Cold-Blooded Penguin*, EBEC
      Funny Feet, Random House, Educational Enrichment
        Materials
      Hector and Christina, EBEC
      Hector Penguin, EBEC

Books: *Which Is Willy?*, Robert Bright
      Your Pet Penguin, Bobbie Hamsa
      Counting Penguins, Caroline Howe
      Tuxedo Sam, Cathy Nichols
      Winston, Newton, Elton and Ed, James Stevenson

Fingerplay: Three Little Penguins. (Source: *Rhymes for Learning Times*, Louise Binder Scott)

Craft: Egg Carton Penguins. Every-day egg cartons can easily be transformed into a delightful penguin with the use of only paint and construction paper. Simply cut one egg carton in half, and paint it black. Use pieces from the other half to create the eyes, beak, and feet.

White construction paper can be used to make the stomach, and then glue it to the front of the egg carton.

For an added touch, sit the creation on a pile of cotton to give the effect of snow. (Source: *Egg Carton Critters*, Donna Miller)

Activity: Animal Walks. This game strengthens children's arms and legs. Select several cards of animal stunts (penguin walk, seal crawl, etc.) where a large part of your weight is on your arms and legs.

Mark out a path for the children to follow while acting out the animal parts. (Source: *Teacher's Handbook of Children's Games*, Marian Jenks Wirth)

23 Birthdays

Filmstrips:	*Ask Mr. Bear*, MacMillan
	A Birthday for Frances, BFA Educational Media
	The Birthday Trombone , EBEC
	Hooper Humperdink..? Not Him, Weston Woods
	Lyle and the Birthday Party, Random House
Films:	*Happy Birthday Moon*, Weston Woods
	A Letter to Amy, Weston Woods
Books:	*Benjamin's 365 Birthdays*, Judi Barrett
	Secret Birthday Message, Eric Carle
	Veronica and the Birthday Present, Roger Duvoisin
	Happy Birthday, Sam, Pat Hutchins
	A Letter to Amy, Ezra Keats

Fingerplay: Look at Me. (Source: *Finger Frolics—Revised*, Liz Cromwell, Dixie Hibner, and John R. Faitel)

Craft: Add-a-Year Candle. Birthdays are important events for children. To help them celebrate their birthday every year, construct a birthday cake for each with a candle that can be added to every year. Cover a box with construction paper and decorate it with flowers and the child's name as you would a cake.

To make a candle, get a cardboard tube (tissue paper roll) and cover it, adding a paper flame to the top. For each year of the child's life, put a strip around the candle with the child's age. This can be added to year after year. (Source: *Purple Cow to the Rescue*, Ann Cole, Carolyn Haas, and Betty Weinberger)

Activity: Musical Parade. Choose a small prize, such as a chocolate bar or a small toy, and wrap it in layers of tissue or wrapping paper. Have the children sit in a circle and pass the gift around the circle. When the music stops that child should remove one layer of wrap. Continue until it is completely uncovered. A similar game is:

Balloon Relay. Divide the class into two groups, each with a box full of inflated balloons. When the signal is given, each team will attempt to burst all their balloons before the opposing team by sitting on them one at a time. (Source: *500 Games*, Peter L. Cave)

Song:	"Happy Birthday to You" (Source: *Singing Bee!: A Collection of Favorite Children's Songs*, Jane Hart)

24 Boats/Ships

Filmstrips: *The Little Red Lighthouse and the Great Gray Bridge*, Weston Woods
Little Tim and the Brave Sea Captain, Weston Woods
Little Toot, Weston Woods
Mr. Gumpy's Outing, Weston Woods
Richard Scarry's Great Steamboat Mystery, Random House

Books: *Who Sank the Boat?*, Pamela Allen
Harbor, Donald Crews
Benjy's Boat Trip, Margaret Graham
Big City Port, Betsy Maestro
Maude and Claude Go Abroad, Susan Meddaugh

Fingerplay: Row the Boat. (Source: *Little Boy Blue*, Daphne Gogstrom)

Craft: Bathtub Boats. A simple boat can be built of clay, paper (sails), toothpicks, and a bottle cap, jar lid, bar of soap, or walnut shell for the base. By using these items for a base, the boat will float which will be the first thing the child will try when he gets his boat near water. Don't disappoint him by using something that won't float. (Source: *Purple Cow to the Rescue*, Ann Cole, Carolyn Haas, and Betty Weinberger)

Activity: Rocking Boat. While singing the song indicated below or "Row the Boat" children may get into pairs. Have two children sit on the floor facing each other. Legs should be spread with feet touching their partners. They may then rock back and forth as a boat would rock. An alternate version can be having the children pretend to row oars and move themselves around the room as if rowing down the river.

Song: "Michael Row the Boat Ashore" (Source: *Do Your Ears Hang Low?*, Tom Glazer)

25 Careers: Dentists/Teeth

Filmstrips: *Crocus*, Random House
Dr. DeSoto, Weston Woods
Heather's Feathers, Random House, Educational
Enrichment Materials
You Can't Put Braces on Spaces, Random House,
Educational Enrichment Materials
A Visit to the Dentist, Walt Disney Educational Media

Books: *The Berenstain Bears Visit the Dentist*, Stan Berenstain
The Dentist's Tools, Carolyn Lapp
Michael and the Dentist, Benard Rockwell
At The Dentist: What Did Christopher See? ,
S. Ziegler

Fingerplay: Brushing Teeth. (Source: *Finger Frolics—Revised*, Liz Cromwell, Dixie Hibner, and John R. Faitel)

Craft: My Tooth Pouch. Using felt, have the children trace and cut out two forms of a tooth. They may then glue eyes on that are easily obtainable at any craft store and put a smile on with markers.

Have the children glue the sides of the tooth together leaving the upper portion open. (Use fabric glue that can be purchased at a craft store.)

The children now own their own tooth holder where they may place their tooth and put under their pillow. The tooth fairy may exchange the tooth for money in the pouch later.

Activity: Good Nutrition. Prepare flashcards or flannel board pictures of different types of foods. Discuss good nutrition and have the children pick out what foods help to make happy teeth.

You might also be able to borrow a dentist's teeth mold to illustrate proper brushing methods. If this is not available to you, try getting a dentist's aide to visit your group and talk to the children.

26 Careers: Firefighters

Filmstrips: *Curious George*, Random House, Educational Enrichment
Materials
Hercules, Weston Woods
I'm No Fool with Fire, Walt Disney Educational Media
Johnny, the Fireman, SVE

Films: *Draghetto*, Phoenix
Helpful Little Fireman, Coronet

Books: *Fireman Jim*, Roger Bester
Clifford's Good Deeds, Norman Bridwell
The Little Fireman, Margaret Wise Brown
A Visit to the Sesame Street Firehouse, Dan Elliott
Fire! Fire!, Gail Gibbons

Fingerplay: Ten Brave Fireman. (Source: *Finger Frolics—Revised*, Liz
Cromwell, Dixie Hibner, and John R. Faitel)

Craft: Firefighters Hat and Ax. Many children get great enjoyment
pretending to be the firemen they see every day on television or in their
neighborhood. The source below gives us instructions on how to make such
things as hats and axes out of cardboard tubes and construction paper.
There are many items related to firefighters that can be made from paper
and boxes.

Instructions are also available for the construction of a firehose, a fire
extinguisher, a fire alarm box, a fire hydrant; an oxygen tank and mask are
also available in the same book and can help to create an entire unit. (Source:
Be What You Want to Be!, Phyllis and Noel Fiarotta)

Activity: Firemen's Visit. Arrange with the local fire department to have
a fire truck visit your school or library so that the firefighters may speak with
the children and show them the tools of the trade.

Many fire departments also arrange visits to the firehouse itself and have
small coloring books on fire safety that they will give you for the children.
Don't forget to make full use of the community services and workers
available in your neighborhood.

Song: "The King and the Fireman" (Source: *People in My
Neighborhood*, Sesame Street Inc.)

27 Careers: Police Officers

Filmstrips: *Make Way for Ducklings*, Weston Woods
People Do Different Kinds of Work, Charlie Brown,
    Random House
You May Like Many Jobs, Charlie Brown, Random House

Film: *Make Way for Ducklings*, Weston Woods

Books: *Who Blew that Whistle?*, Leone Adelson
Someone Always Needs a Policeman, David Brown
My Dog Is Lost!, Ezra Keats
Policeman Small, Lois Lenski
I Can be a Police Officer, Catherine Mathias

Fingerplay: Traffic Policeman. (Source: *Finger Frolics—Revised*, Liz Cromwell, Dixie Hibner, and John R. Faitel)

Craft: The Funny Police Officer. Police officers are described to children as the people to look for when they're lost or need help. An officer should never be portrayed as someone to be feared. To help the child have a good feeling about police officers, why not make masks and allow them to act out what they believe the police do. In the book below you will find instructions for making just such a mask out of construction paper, oaktag, markers, and glue. This particular policeman sports a beard and a bobby hat. (Source: *Great Masks to Make*, Robyn Supraner)

If you would like to add more to the craft and expand your career unit try making the badge, policeman's hat, handcuffs, night stick, ticket book, traffic signs, and traffic lights shown in this source: (Source: *Be What You Want to Be!*, Phyllis and Noel Fiarotta)

Activity: Police Safety Program. Invite the local police department to send a representative to speak to the children about their job and to encourage the children to look to the police for help when they need it. The local police departments can usually be counted on to speak to parents and children at programs on the following topics:

- Strangers
- Bicycle and Traffic Safety
- Dangers of Drugs
- Fingerprinting of Children

Song: "The Traffic Cop" (Source: *This is Music; Book 2,* William R. Sur)

28 Character Traits: Kindness

Filmstrips: *Andy and the Lion,* Weston Woods
The Biggest Bear, Weston Woods
Horton Hatches an Egg, Random House
Theodore, BFA Educational Media

Books: *The Happy Hunter,* Roger Duvoisin
Jennie's Hat, Ezra Jack Keats
Clotilda, Jack Kent
If You Give a Mouse a Cookie, Laura Numeroff
I Know a Lady, Charlotte Zolotow

Fingerplay: Being Kind. (Source: *Finger Frolics—Revised,* Liz Cromwell, Dixie Hibner, and John R. Faitel)

Craft: Certificates of Kindness. After a discussion on what services the children can perform to be kind and helpful to their parents, try creating a certificate booklet. Let the children select two or three services they would like to do for their parents (sweep the floor, make a bed, help dad wash the car, etc.). Distribute drawing paper and crayons to the children and allow them to draw themselves doing chores for their parents. Because of the age of the children you will have to write the accompanying phrase describing the pictures (Ex: wash the dishes, make my bed).

After each is done, design a cover and staple the coupons together alone with a note to the parents:

Dear Mom and Dad:
You always help me with so many things. Now it's my turn. Here are some coupons for you to use when you need help. Pick the one you need help with, and give it to me. I promise to help you then.
Love,

Activity: Come on and Join in the Game. A physical activity song which allows the children time for movement during the storyhour session. (Source: *The Fireside Book of Children's Songs,* Marie Winn)

Song: "Be Kind to Your Webfooted Friends" (Source: *The Fireside Song Book of Birds and Beasts,* Jane Yolen)

29 Circus and Circus Animals

Filmstrips: *C is for Clown*, Random House
The Circus Baby, Weston Woods
Curious George Rides a Bike, Weston Woods
If I Ran the Circus, Random House
Harry the Hider, Imperial Educational Resources

Books: *Bearymore*, Don Freeman
Henrietta, Circus Star, Syd Hoff
Harriet Goes to the Circus, Betsy and Giulio Maestro
Liverwurst Is Missing, Mercer Mayer
Smallest Elephant in the World, Alvin Tresselt

Fingerplay: Ten Circus Wagons. (Source: *Finger Frolics—Revised*, Liz Cromwell, Dixie Hibner, and John R. Faitel)

Craft: Dancing Clown. Precut pieces are suggested for this craft. Pages 46 and 47 of the book listed below can be copied on a copy machine to help make patterns for each of these pieces. A bright and amusing clown can be constructed out of inexpensive materials such as construction paper, tape, markers, glue, and rubberbands. The source below will give you full instructions along with a full-page, color illustration of how your final product should look. The hands and shoes are connected to the body with rubber bands. A rubberband is also attached to the top of the hat so that you can bounce the clown up and down. I suggest that the top rubberband be connected to a stick for easier handling. (Source: *Rainy Day Surprises You Can Make*, Robyn Supraner)

Activity: Be a Clown. As suggested in the book below you might wish to connect this song and activity with a session of face painting to make the children look and feel like clowns.

Now, with the use of the music and verses given in the book, the children will get a chance to act like clowns. The song also lends itself easily to further suggestions from the children on what clowns do. Often they can come up with better suggestions than we can, and it makes for a more enjoyable program. (Source: *Game-Songs with Prof Dogg's Troupe*, Harriet Powell)

Song: "The Man on the Flying Trapeze" (Source: *The Man on the Flying Trapeze*, Robert Quackenbush)

30 Clothing

Filmstrips:	*Corduroy*, Live Oak Media
	The Emperor's New Clothes, Britannica Learning Materials
	Funny Feet, Random House, Educational Enrichment Materials
	No Roses for Harry, Random House
	Old Hat, New Hat, Random House
Films:	*Charlie Needs a Cloak*, Weston Woods
	A Pocket for Corduroy, Phoenix
Books:	*Tan Tan's Hat*, Kazuo Iwamura
	Jennie's Hat, Ezra Keats
	Katy No-Pocket, Emmy Payne
	Caps for Sale, Esphyr Slobodkina
	Max's New Suit, Rosemary Wells

Fingerplay: My Zipper Suit. (Source: *Finger Frolics—Revised*, Liz Cromwell, Dixie Hibner, and John R. Faitel)

Craft: String a Necklace or Headbands. Children enjoy stringing various items. Beaded necklaces can be made by stringing macaroni, paper, or straw beads on kite string. The straw beads can be cut in various lengths from drinking straws and colored with markers. For a better variety of shapes and sizes try shapes from construction paper and stringing them through holes in the center. Macaroni also is available in different sizes and shapes. To add color here you might try food coloring.

Headbands lend themselves to more creative decorations as is illustrated in the book indicated here. (Source: *Sticks and Stones and Ice Cream Cones*, Phyllis Fiarotta)

Activity and Song: The Mulberry Bush. The music book listed here will supply you with the sheet music for this song which could be played by piano or guitar. All eight verses are supplied, the basic verse and seven verses pertaining to the days of the week. Have the children repeat the verses you sing. When they are comfortable with the words and music, you may add the body motions for acting out the verse. (Source: *Singing Bee!: A Collection of Favorite Children's Songs*, Jane Hart)

31 Clothing: Hats

Filmstrips: *Caps for Sale*, Weston Woods
Cat in the Hat, Random House
The Hat, Weston Woods
How the Trollusk Got His Hat, Listening Library
Old Hat, New Hat, Random House

Books: *Martin's Hat*, Jean Blos
The 500 Hats of Bartholomew Cubbins, Theodor Geisel
Tan Tan's Hat, Kazuo Iwamura
Jennie's Hat, Ezra Keats
The Horse with the Easter Bonnet, Catherine Wooley

Fingerplay: Special Hats. (Source: *Rhymes for Learning Times*, Louise Binder Scott)

Craft: Party Hats. Dress up and pretend are common activities with the children at the preschool age level. Young children also seem to have an uninhibited imagination for making things that, unfortunately, some of us lose as we grow older.

Party hats can be designed by using paper plates or foil pie plates for the base. Trimmings for the hat can be left largely to the imagination, but you will have to guide some. Use materials you have available, such as, crepe paper, stickers, doilies, ribbon, yarn, feathers, or even buttons and more. (Source: *I Saw a Purple Cow*, Ann Cole, Carolyn Haas, Faith Bushnell, and Betty Weinberger)

Activity: Musical Hats. This is a variation on Musical Chairs with all players sitting in a circle. All players are given a hat except one. While the music plays everyone passes the hats around the circle trying each one on in turn. When the music stops the child without a hat on is out of the game.

The choice of music is left solely to your choice depending on the age of the group. Suggestion: Try nursery songs they are all familiar with so they can sing along. (Source: *500 Games*, Peter L. Cave)

Song: "My Tall Silk Hat" (Source: *Do Your Ears Hang Low?*, Tom Glazer)

32 Concepts: Color

Filmstrips: *Freight Train*, Random House, Educational Enrichment
Materials
Harold and the Purple Crayon, Weston Woods
Oh, Were They Ever Happy, Listening Library
Roses Are Red, Are Violets Blue?, Random House
Under the Rainbow, Random House, Miller-Brody

Film: *Little Blue and Little Yellow*, McGraw

Books: *The Mixed-Up Chameleon*, Eric Carle
The Chalk Box Story, Don Freeman
Mr. Pine's Purple House, Leonard Kessler
Put Me in the Zoo, Robert Lopshire
The Big Orange Splot, Daniel Pinkwater

Craft: Story Pictures. In conjunction with *The Chalkbox Story* by Don Freeman listed above, the children may be given black construction paper and colored chalk to create their own picture as they have seen in the story read to them.

These pictures may later be displayed in the library or classroom.

Activity and Song: Parade of Colors. The children identify ten colors (blue, red, black, green, yellow, pink, purple, brown, white and orange). They are each given a card with a color and instructed to march in a circle until their color is mentioned and told to either sit down or stand up.

This is a very basic concept activity that young children can handle easily. (Source: *Learning Basic Skills Through Music, V. 2*, Hap Palmer)

33 Concepts: Shapes

Filmstrips: *Old Hat, New Hat*, Random House
Sam Shape and the Clumsy Car, Clearvue
Shapelessville "Shapes Up", Clearvue
The Shape of Me and Other Stuff, Random House

Books: *Ten Black Dots*, Donald Crews
Circles, Triangles and Squares, Tana Hoban
The Emperor's Oblong Pancake, Peter Hughes
It Looked Like Spilt Milk, Charles Shaw
The Missing Piece, Shel Silverstein

Fingerplay: Draw A Circle. (Source: *Finger Frolics—Revised*, Liz Cromwell, Dixie Hibner, and John R. Faitel)

Crafts: My Shape Book and Felt Pictures. After discussing the basic shapes of circle, square, triangle, and rectangle, help the children develop their own book of shapes. Have precut patterns of the shapes available for the children to trace. Then distribute sheets of rough sandpaper on which the children can trace these shapes and cut them out. Some children will need help with the cutting while others will be able to accomplish this task alone.

Have all the sandpaper shapes mounted on colored construction paper and stapled together with a decorative cover to form the child's own shape book. The result is a book in which a child can recognize and feel the shapes discussed and later learn the terms if you print them under each shape. Or, make a felt board for each child by gluing a piece of black felt 9 inches by 12 inches to a piece of cardboard the same size. Give each child various pieces of light-colored felt cut in the basic shapes discussed. Using these pieces, demonstrate how to design a picture with them while the children copy it or design their own. (Source: *More Beginning Crafts for Beginning Readers*, Alice Gilbreath)

Activity: Hoopla. Circular rings may be used here to toss on pegs to score points in this game. Suggestion: To adapt this game, shapes may be placed on the gameboard instead of numbers and children may score by ringing chosen shapes. (Source: *Games*, Caroline Pitcher)

Song: "Footprints" (Source: *Monsters and Monstrous Things,* Upbeat Basics Cassettes, P.O. Box 120516, Acklen Station, Nashville, TN 37212)

34 Concepts: Size

Filmstrips: *Big Dog...Little Dog*, Random House
The Biggest House in the World, Random House
Old Hat, New Hat, Random House
The Story of Little Thumb, EBEC
Thumbelina, Live Oak Media

Books: *Little Elephant and Big Mouse*, Benita Cantieni
Is It Red? Is It Yellow? Is It Blue?, Tana Hoban
The Biggest Fish in the Sea, Dahlov Ipcar
The Little Giant, Robert Kraus
Sizes, Jan Pienkowski

Fingerplay: Small and Tall. (Source: *Rhymes for Learning Times*, Louise Binder Scott)

Craft: The Three Bears Puppets. Have the children trace ready-made patterns or cookie cutters to make the form of the three bears at different sizes. They may then decorate and cut them out by putting on the eyes, nose, and pads for the paws. If time permits, you may cut short pieces of brown yarn to make the body fuzzy.

When completed, put the bears on sticks and have the children act out the story of *The Three Bears*.

Activity: Sometimes I'm Tall. This is a blindfold game. These types of games can be used to help develop a child's hearing perceptions and awareness of the concepts of small and tall.

Select one child to be "It." Blindfold the child with his or her back to the group. The remainder of the children can either stand in a circle or scatter loosely across the opposite side of the room.

With the guidance of the teacher, the children can recite the given verse (text in book below) about being small and tall as they squat down or stand tall. At the end of the verse the blindfolded child can guess if everyone is tall or small. If he correctly guesses he may change places with another child. (Source: *Teacher's Handbook of Children's Games*, Marian Jenks Wirth)

35 Counting

Filmstrips:	*Bears on Wheels*, Random House
	Lentil Soup, Weston Woods
	Little Monster's Counting Book, Listening Library
	One Was Johnny, Weston Woods
	Ten Apples Up on Top, Random House
Films:	*Over in the Meadow*, Weston Woods
	Really Rosie, Weston Woods
	The Shout It Out Alphabet Film, Phoenix
Books:	*Ten, Nine, Eight*, Molly Bang
	Twenty-two Bears, Claire Bishop
	Ten Black Dots, Donald Crews
	Roll Over!, Mordicai Gerstein
	Harriet Goes to the Circus, Betsy Maestro

Fingerplay: Tall Fence Posts. (Source: *Rhymes for Learning Times*, Louise Binder Scott)

Craft and Activity: Dominoes. Dominoes is a simple enough game to play with children three to five years of age. It has the advantage of being a game that can be played in a quiet area and with as many children as you like.

The children can be helped in making their own set of dominoes in various ways:

- Use cut pieces of cardstock or cardboard and use colored sticker dots to add color to each.

- Using the same background, cut sandpaper for dots so that they can be felt as well as seen.

- In place of dots cut out numerals in different colored paper to be glued to the dominoes.

- If you don't want each child to make their own set, have them co-operate in making one giant set for the library or classroom using poster board. Let each domino be one foot by two feet in size. They might wish to paint on the dots or numerals.

Song:	"One, two, three, four, five" (Source: *Sing Hey Diddle, Diddle*, Beatrice Harrop)

36 Days of the Week, Months of the Year

Filmstrips: *Chicken Soup with Rice,* Weston Woods
May Day: The Merry Month of May, Walt Disney
  Educational Media
The Merry Mouse Book of Months, SVE
One Monday Morning, Weston Woods

Film: *Really Rosie,* Weston Woods

Books: *The Very Hungry Caterpillar,* Eric Carle
Lentil Soup, Joe Lasker
Wise Owl's Days of the Week, Moncure
The Tale of Georgie Grub, Jeanne Willis
No Bath Tonight, Jane Yolen

Fingerplay: During the Week. (Source: *Rhymes for Learning Times,* Louise Binder Scott)

Craft: Calendar Bingo. Bingo is a favorite game for many people and this simple game can be adapted by using the days of the week. The boards can be made of cardstock or posterboard. Replace the letters B-I-N-G-O with the words for the days of the week. Since you only have five letters in Bingo to be replaced you might want to differentiate between weekdays and weekend days.

For children just learning to recognize the days of the week, have the parts made up beforehand and have them copy a sample board displayed.

Bingo chips can be any number of objects such as buttons, pebbles, pennies, etc.

Activity: Calendar Toss. The gameboard for this activity is obviously a page from a calendar. If you feel that the calendars you have available make too small a board, you might want to make a larger version using a piece of large posterboard.

Place the board on the floor and give each child a given number of markers to toss on the board. The markers can be pebbles, buttons, etc.

The game can be played any number of ways:
- Have young children try to hit a particular date.
- Have older children try to add up the dates hit for the highest score total.
- Try dividing teams to hit odd or even numbers.

(Source: *I Saw A Purple Cow*, Ann Cole, Carolyn Haas, Faith Bushnell, and Betty Weinberger)

Song: "Round the Mulberry Bush" (Source: *Singing Bee!: A Collection of Favorite Children's Songs*, Jane Hart)

37 Dinosaurs

Filmstrips: *Danny and the Dinosaur*, Weston Woods
Dinny and Danny, MacMillan
Dinosaur Tales: Baby Horned-Faced and the Egg Stealer, Coronet
Mr. Terwilliger's Secret, Random House, Educational Enrichment Materials

Film: *The Mysterious Tadpole*, Weston Woods

Books: *If the Dinosaurs Came Back*, Bernard Most
Dinosaurs Do's and Don'ts, Jean Polhamus
What Did the Dinosaurs Eat?, Wilda Ross
Mitchell Is Moving, Marjorie Sharmat
Quiet on Account of Dinosaurs, Catherine Woolley

Fingerplay: Ten Huge Dinosaurs. (Source: *Rhymes for Learning Times*, Louise Binder Scott)

Craft: Scale a Dinosaur. There are a number of types of dinosaurs that children can be introduced to with hard shells, scales, or spikes. Choose one of these types and have a form run off on cardstock for the children. Give them paper to cut out scales that can then be glued to the body. If time permits you might want to do a variety of dinosaurs and staple them together for a dinosaur book.

You can also trace the figure of a dinosaur on paper large enough to cover a wall or window. Have the children trace and cut out different colored scales to decorate the creature. This may be a project that a whole school or community may want to become involved in. Have each child write his name on the scale he creates.

Activity and Song: When a Dinosaur's Feeling Hungry. This is a simple acting-out song. Dinosaurs are an ever-popular topic with children of all ages. Here you will find the source for the music and verses to the song "When a Dinosaur's Feeling Hungry." Begin with a discussion on what the children think dinosaurs would like to eat and what they wouldn't like. At this point you might talk about meat-eaters versus plant-eaters.

Insert the children's suggestions in the appropriate spaces in the song, and let the children act as if they are the dinosaurs while they sing the song. (Source: *Game-Songs with Prof Dogg's Troupe*, Harriet Powell)

38 Dragons

Filmstrips: *Custard the Dragon,* Weston Woods
Frog and Toad Together: Dragons and Giants, Random
    House
Pete's Dragon, Walt Disney Educational Media
The Reluctant Dragon, Walt Disney Educational Media
Seasonal Adventures of the Lollipop Dragon, SVE

Films: *Draghetto,* Phoenix
Dragon Stew, Phoenix
Puff, the Magic Dragon, Coronet

Books: *The Funny Thing,* Wanda Gag
The Once-Upon-a-Time Dragon, Jack Kent
There's No Such Thing as a Dragon, Jack Kent
The Dragon Who Lived Downstairs, Burr Tillstrom
Everyone Knows What a Dragon Looks Like, Jay
    Williams

Fingerplay: Little Huey Dragon. (Source: *Finger Frolics—Revised,* Liz
Cromwell, Dixie Hibner, and John R. Faitel)

Craft: The Dragon Mask. Children love to pretend they are large, mythical
creatures, and dragons are right up there at the top of the list with dinosaurs.
Let the children develop their own dragon mask using a large, brown
(paper) grocery bag. Most parents would even have a bag at home that the
child can bring in with him.

Use construction paper to make the dragon's eyes, ears, scales, mouth,
and a tongue that hangs out of the mouth. The book by Robyn Supraner
gives you two full-page illustrations of how this mask could look.

Upon completion of this craft have the children wear them on their head
while they play "Dragon Tag" described below. (Source: *Great Masks to
Make,* Robyn Supraner)

Activity: Dragon Tag. This game requires at least ten players or more.
While four form a chain to become the dragon, they attempt to capture the
other players without losing the chain. As each player is tagged (captured),
he links up with the chain to become part of the dragon. (Source: *Games,*
Anne Rockwell)

Song: "Puff the Magic Dragon" (Source: *The Reader's Digest Children's
Songbook,* Wiliam L. Simon)

39 Ecology

Filmstrips: *The Butter Battle Book,* Random House
The Little House, Walt Disney Educational Media
The Lorax, Random House
The Neatos and the Litterbugs, Random House, Miller-Brody

Books: *Happy Hunter,* Roger Duvoisin
Grizzwold, Sydney Hoff
The Caboose Who Got Lose, Bill Peet
Andy and the Wild Ducks, Mayo Short
Edith and Little Bear Lend a Hand, Dare Wright

Fingerplay: Fire, Earth, Water and Air. (Source: *Finger Frolics—Revised,* Liz Cromwell, Dixie Hibner, and John R. Faitel)

Craft: Egg Carton Wastebasket. Collect egg cartons (styrofoam ones, if possible) to make a small wastebasket for the child's room. These can be used as the sides of the basket and can be painted unless you are able to obtain the egg cartons that are already in colors. An aluminum foil pan (the bottom), plastic bag and yarn will also be needed.

This craft could be followed by having the children go on a walking tour of the grounds to beautify their school, library, or township. (Source: *Do a Zoom-Do,* Bernice Chesler)

Activity: The Litterbug. This game is a variation of "Duck, Duck, Goose" and should be preceded by a discussion that we are all responsible for keeping our community clean. This can encompass as many children as you may need. Have all the children stand in a circle facing inward except one, the Litterbug. The Litterbug walks around the exterior of the circle until he drops a piece of paper, can, or other item designated behind one child.

The child in the circle who has the "garbage" dropped by him picks it up and attempts to return it to the Litterbug by tagging him with it before he gets around the circle and back to the empty spot. If he succeeds, he returns to the circle, if not, he becomes the Litterbug.

40 Emotions

Filmstrips: *Alexander and the Wind-up Mouse,* Weston Woods
                 Corduroy, Live Oak Media
                 The Happy Owls, Random House
                 There's a Nightmare in My Closet, Weston Woods

Film: *Louis James Hates School,* LCA

Books: *The Bravest Babysitter,* Barbara Greenberg
                 A Baby Sister for Frances, Russell Hoban
                 The Lady Who Saw the Good Side of Everything, Pat
                     Tapio
                 I Love My Mother, Paul Zindel
                 The Quarreling Book, Charlotte Zolotow

Fingerplay: When I Am.... (Source: *Finger Frolics—Revised,* Liz Cromwell, Dixie Hibner, and John R. Faitel)

Craft: Happy/Sad Face Stick Puppets. The children can construct a reversible face puppet to help them display the emotions they feel. Using a paper plate, have the children draw a sad face on one side with crayons or markers and a happy face on the opposite side. Give them some yarn to glue to the top and sides of the paper plate to form the hair.

     Mount the plate on a popsicle stick for ease of handling.

Activity: Feelings. During a discussion of how children feel about different situations, the children may use their new mask puppets to demonstrate their answers by holding them up to their faces.

     As you read some of the stories listed above to the children, let them use their masks to express the feelings of the characters in the tale.

Song: "If You're Happy and You Know It..." (Source: *The Reader's Digest Children's Songbook,* Wiliam L. Simon)

41 Ethnic Groups in the U.S.: Native Americans

Filmstrips: *The Fire Stealer*, Oxford University Press
How Mother Possum Got Her Pouch, Britannica
Learning Materials
How to Woodpecker Got His Feathers, Britannica
Learning Materials
Little Burnt Face, Britannica Learning Materials

Books: *Little Owl Indian*, Hetty Beatty
Red Fox and His Canoe, Nathaniel Benchley
Indian Bunny, Ruth Bornstein
The Legend of Bluebonnet, Tomie dePaola
One Little Indian, Grace Moon

Fingerplay: Ten Little Indians. (Source: *Games for the Very Young*, Elizabeth Matterson)

Craft: Shield Decorations. Shields are a special part of the American Indian culture. A simple shield can be made by cutting two large circles (one smaller than the other) out of colored posterboard. Glue the smaller one to the center of the larger, and add string to the back for holding the shield.

Additional ornaments can be added to the inner or outer circles by drawing and cutting out paper arrows, suns, tepees, etc. Feathers can be glued to the bottom to hang below the shield. Make one for each nation you study. (Source: *Confetti: The Kids' Make-It-Yourself, Do-It-Yourself Party Book*, Phyllis and Noel Fiarotta)

Activity: Indian Chief. Players sit in a circle, facing one another. One child must leave the room or be blindfolded. Another child is made chief. The chief will perform actions (clap hands, etc.) which the tribe must repeat quickly. The first child returns and must determine who the chief is while the group performs. (Source: *500 Games*, Peter L. Cave)

Song: "Ten Little Indians" (Source: *Eye Winker, Tom Tinker, Chin Chopper*, Tom Glazer)

42 Fairy Tales and Nursery Rhymes

Filmstrips: *Cinderella,* Walt Disney Educational Media
The Gingerbread Boy, Coronet
Henny Penny, Coronet
Little Red Riding Hood, SVE
Rumplestiltskin, EBEC

Films: *Harold's Fairy Tale,* Weston Woods
The Ugly Duckling, Weston Woods
Wynken, Blynken and Nod, Weston Woods

Books: *The Three Billy Goats Gruff,* Peter Asbjornsen
The Three Bears, Paul Galdone
The Three Little Pigs, Paul Galdone
The Hare and the Tortoise, Jean de LaFontaine
Puss in Boots, Charles Perrault

Fingerplay: Little Jack Horner. (Source: *Finger Frolics—Revised,* Liz Cromwell, Dixie Hibner, and John R. Faitel)

Craft: The Gingerbread Man. Following the readings of *The Gingerbread Man,* let the children make their own man out of construction paper. Distribute brown construction paper and precut patterns or use large cookie cutters of the gingerbread man to be traced. After tracing and cutting these forms out, you can decorate the cookie in one of two suggested ways:

- Use colored chalk as icing to draw clothes on and sticker dots for eyes, nose, and buttons.

- Cut clothes out of paper and glue it on. Use real raisins or small hard candies for eyes, nose, and buttons.

(NOTE: Emphasize that the food is decorative and not edible.)

Activity: The Trolls and the Kids. Read the story of *The Three Billy Goats Gruff* to the children. Discuss key points in the story, such as, the rickety bridge, a cave, the troll, etc. You can then prepare to act out the story by constructing a bridge of chairs with poles across them (some low and some high). A cave can be made of a small barrel or a sheet thrown over a table.

Use a drum to make the sounds of the trolls. The children may cross the bridge by crawling under the high bars and stepping over the low ones only when the drum sounds. They must freeze in mid-air when it stops.

Be careful to avoid awakening the trolls by rattling the poles and then being captured. (Source: *Teacher's Handbook of Children's Games*, Marian Jenks Wirth)

Song: "Baa, Baa, Black Sheep" (Source: *Singing Bee!: A Collection of Favorite Children's Songs*, Jane Hart)

43 Family Life: Mothers

Filmstrips: *Are You My Mother?*, Random House
The Best Mom in the World, Random House, Educational
Enrichment Materials
The Day After Mother's Day, Eye Gate Media
Lollipop Dragon's Mother's Day, SVE
Mothers Can Do Anything, Imperial Educational
Resources

Books: *Bread and Honey*, Frank Asch
Ask Mr. Bear, Marjorie Flack
Joey, Jack Kent
Mother, Mother I Want Another, Maria Polushkin
I Love My Mother, Paul Zindel

Fingerplay: My Whole Family. (Source: *Finger Frolics—Revised*, Liz
Cromwell, Dixie Hibner, and John R. Faitel)

Craft: Seeded Pencil Holder. Any small can can be made into a beautiful
pencil holder for mom on Mother's Day. Collect various types of seeds
(melon, bird, sunflower, etc.) to add variety to the design. Rather than
trying to glue the seeds directly to the can itself, Phyllis Fiarotta, in her book,
suggests cutting a piece of paper to fit the exterior of the can, then laying the
paper flat to add the seeds.

A decorated can of this sort can be used for crayons, or even mom's or
dad's pencils, needles, or more. For step-by-step illustrated directions take
a look at Fiarotta's book listed here. (Source: *Snips and Snails and Walnut
Whales*, Phyllis Fiarotta)

Activity: Mother, May I?. This simple game can be played with any
number of children. One player (Mother) stands at one side of the room
while the other players stand at the other side. The leader states how many
steps the children may take to try to reach her. The players must ask her,
"Mother, may I?" *before* moving or they return to the beginning of their trip.

Song: "Mother's Day" (Source: *God's Wonderful World*, Agnes Leckie
Mason and Phyllis Brown Ohanian)
or
"Mother Hen" (Source: *Singing Time: A Book of Songs for
Little Children*, Satis N. Coleman and Alice G. Thorn)

44 Farms

Filmstrips: *Henny Penny*, Coronet
The Little Red Hen, Coronet
Petunia, Beware, Random House
The Turnip, MacMillan

Films: *The Little Rooster Who Made the Sun Rise*, Coronet
Rosie's Walk, Weston Woods

Books: *Big Red Barn*, Margaret Wise Brown
Crocus, Roger Duvoisin
Who Took the Farmer's Hat?, Joan Lexau
Hamilton, Robert Peck
Emmett's Pig, Mary Stolz

Fingerplay: The Scarecrow. (Source: *Little Boy Blue*, Daphne Hogstrom)

Craft: Farm Animals: Sheep. Discuss different animals that can be found on a farm with the children. In the source below a large full-page illustration (8-1/2"x11") of a sheep may duplicated onto cardstock. The children can be given cotton balls to glue to the sheep to give it the soft texture it should have. (Source: *The Kid's Stuff Book of Patterns, Projects and Plans*, Imogene Forte)

Activity: Feathers, Feathers. This game requires a minimum of five players but can include as many children over five that you may need. The chosen leader begins by saying the name of the game and an animal with feathers, duck feathers, turkey feathers, etc.). He also begins flapping around like a chicken. Other players also flap their arms. The leader continues to call out naming animals with feathers until he suddenly includes one that doesn't have feathers (pig, cow, sheep, etc.). Any players still flapping at this point are out of the game. (Source: *Games*, Anne Rockwell)

Song: "Old MacDonald Had a Farm" (Source: *Eye Winker, Tom Tinker, Chin Chopper*, Tom Glazer)

45 Fish

Filmstrips: *Fish Is Fish*, Random House
A Fish Out of Water, Random House
McElligot's Pool, Random House
One Fish, Two Fish, Red Fish, Blue Fish, Random House
Swimmy, Random House

Films: *The Fisherman and His Wife*, Weston Woods
How the Whale Got His Throat, Coronet
Jonah and the Great Fish, Weston Woods

Books: *A Fish Hatches*, Joanna Cole
The Biggest Fish in the Sea, Dahlov Ipcar
Lorenzo, Benard Waber
Brian Wildsmith's Fishes, Brian Wildsmith
Louis the Fish, Arthur Yorinks

Fingerplay: Three Little Fish. (Source: *Finger Frolics—Revised*, Liz Cromwell, Dixie Hibner, and John R. Faitel)

Craft: Paper-Bag Fish. A small lunch bag, crayons, and colored paper can easily be made into a stuffed fish—one end closed and spread for the tail. Then add scales and fins to the bag. Scales can be made of large stickers or small fins cut out of construction paper and glued on.

For an added touch, attach the fish to a string and a stick to form a fishing pole. (Source: *Easy Art Lessons, K-6*, Tyyne Straatviel and Carolyn K. Corl)

Activity: Catching a Fish. Divide the room with the use of a rope or tape. Children stand in half of the room (the river) and the leader is the farmer trying to catch fish to stock his pond (other half of the room). The leader will give the fish actions to perform while the tom-tom beats, but when it stops everyone must freeze. The last two to freeze must cross the room to the pond and be added to the farmer's stock.

This game can help develop a child's ability to follow directions, his balance, and reactions. Any variety of skills can be incorporated into this game making a lesson an enjoyable time. (Source: *Teacher's Handbook of Children's Games*, Marian Jenks Wirth)

Song: "Three Little Fishes" (Source: *The Reader's Digest Children's Songbook*, Wiliam L. Simon)

46 Food and Eating

Filmstrips: *Andrew and the Strawberry Monster,* EBEC
The Big Honey Hunt, Random House
Chicken Soup with Rice, Weston Woods
Green Eggs and Ham, Random House
I Know an Old Lady Who Swallowed a Fly, Listening
Library

Films: *Dragon Stew,* Phoenix
Frog Goes to Dinner, Phoenix
Stone Soup, Weston Woods

Books: *Cloudy with a Chance of Meatballs,* Judi Barrett
The Turnip, Janina Domanska
The Gingerbread Boy, Paul Galdone
The Magic Porridge Pot, Paul Galdone
The Fat Cat, Jack Kent

Fingerplay: Pancake. (Source: *Children's Counting-Out Rhymes, Finger-plays, Jump-Rope and Bounce-Ball Chants and Other Rhythms,* Gloria T. Delamar)

Craft: Decorative Boxes and Pretty Jewelry. With the use of the great variety of grains and pasta available, the children can make their own jewelry or decorate a colorful box to be used for almost anything. Instructions and illustrations for these crafts can be found in the source below. Suggested grains to use include maize, rice, lentils, pearl barley, macaroni, spaghetti, butterfly pasta and vermicelli. (Source: *The Fun-To-Make Book,* Colette Lamargue)

Activity: The Fat Cat. After reading Jack Kent's *The Fat Cat,* have the children join in acting out the story. The teacher or librarian may drape a long sheet or blanket around herself. As the story progresses and the children take their parts, they will go under the blanket as they are eaten by the cat.

Song: "On Top of Spaghetti" (Source: *Glory, Glory, How Peculiar,* Charles Keller)

47 Foreign Lands: Africa

Filmstrip: *The Iguana Who Was Always Right*, Britannica
                Learning Materials

Films: *A Story, A Story*, Weston Woods
                How the Leopard Got Its Spots, Coronet
                Why Mosquitoes Buzz in People's Ears, Weston Woods

Books: *Rosebud*, Ludwig Bemelmans
                The Happy Lion in Africa, Louise Fatio
                Mother Crocodile, Rosa Guy
                The Tale of a Crocodile, Ann Kirn
                Anansi the Spider, Gerald McDermott

Fingerplay: This Little Tiger. (Source: *Finger Frolics—Revised*, Liz Cromwell, Dixie Hibner, and John R. Faitel)

Craft: African Drum. Using any cylinder-shaped box, such as, an oatmeal box—cut the top and bottom out to make the sides of the drum. These parts will be replaced with pieces of felt and sewn on with yarn.

Decorative designs can be added by using poster paints, crayons, and feathers. The results of your work will give you a workable musical instrument. (Source: *101 Easy Art Activities*, Trudy Aarons and Francine Doelsch or *Sticks and Stones and Ice Cream Cones*, Phyllis Fiarotta)

Activity: Kasha Mu Bukondi or Antelope in the Net. One player is selected to be the antelope and is surrounded by a net (circle) of children. Everyone holds hands and shouts "Kasha Mu Bukondi" and the antelope will try to break through the net. When he successfully escapes, he is chased and the one who captures him becomes the new antelope. (Source: *This Way to Books*, Caroline Feller Bauer)

Song: "Walking Through the Jungle" (Source: *Game-Songs with Prof Dogg's Troupe*, Harriet Powell)

48 Foreign Lands: China

Filmstrips: *The Five Chinese Brothers*, Weston Woods
King of the Forest, Britannica Learning Materials
The Monkey King, SVE
The Story of Ping, Weston Woods
Tikki Tikki Tembo, Weston Woods

Film: *The Five Chinese Brothers*, Weston Woods

Books: *Ming Lo Moves the Mountain*, Arnold Lobel
Teddy Bear and the Chinese Dragon, Jan Mogensen
Tubby and the Lantern, Al Perkins
Everyone Knows What a Dragon Looks Like, Jay
    Williams
The Emperor and the Kite, Jane Yolen

Craft: Bing-Banger Noisemaker. This small Chinese toy is constructed of corrugated cardboard, string, crayons, metal washers or beads, and a pencil. It is a simple toy that can be held in small hands and spun back-and-forth to make the desired noise.

A circular piece of corrugated cardboard can be painted or colored in any pattern desired, and then mounted on a pencil. With a bead on a string attached to two sides of the circle, you can spin the pencil to make the beads bounce off the cardboard.

This toy was made popular again in the film *Karate Kid II* which many children have seen. (Source: *Confetti: The Kids' Make-It-Yourself, Do-It-Yourself Party Book*, Phyllis and Noel Fiarotta)

Activity: Clapping Hands. This clapping game is played similarly to that of "Pease Porridge Hot." It may take some practice with the group but this is a game they will enjoy and practice long after the storyhour program has ended. The actual text of "Pease Porridge Hot" can be located on page 31 of Vinton's book. (Source: *The Folkways Omnibus of Children's Games*, Iris Vinton)

49 Friendship

Suggestion: Use this during Brotherhood Week

Filmstrips: *Mousekin Finds a Friend,* Random House, Miller-Brody
The Three Funny Friends, Random House, Educational
　　Enrichment Materials
Thy Friend Obadiah, Viking Press
Timothy Goes to School, Weston Woods
The Worst Person in the World, Imperial Educational
　　Resources

Films: *Ira Sleeps Over,* Phoenix
Peter's Chair, Weston Woods

Books: *Do You Want to be My Friend?,* Eric Carle
May I Bring a Friend?, Beatrice deRegniers
Timothy Turtle, Al Graham
Little Blue and Little Yellow, Leo Lionni
Little Bear's Friend, Else Minarik

Fingerplay: **Five Friends.** (Source: *Children's Counting-Out Rhymes, Fingerplays, Jump-Rope and Bounce-Ball Chants and Other Rhythms,* Gloria T. Delamar)

Craft: A Friendship Chain. Have each child cut a strip of construction paper (2"x8" long). To this strip have them glue or draw three pictures of things they like to do with others.

All the links designed may be connected to form a friendship chain with each child's name to display in the library during Brotherhood Week.

Activity: A Lonely Little Ghost. Choose one child to be the lonely ghost. Mark an area with tape on the floor for his home. The other children will try to sneak into the area to tease the ghost while reciting a simple verse about the ghost friend. (Text found on page 71 of the book.) Any child tagged will become the ghost's friend and will help to catch the others. The last one tagged wins the game. (Source: *New Games to Play,* Juel Krisvoy)

Song: "Buddies and Pals" (Source: *Do Your Ears Hang Low?,* Tom
　　Glazer)

50 Frogs and Toads

Filmstrips: *Emil, the Tap Dancing Frog*, EBEC
The Foolish Frog, Weston Woods
Frog and Toad are Friends: The Story, Random
House, Miller-Brody
The Frog Prince, Imperial Film Company
Would You Rather Be a Bullfrog?, Random House

Films: *A Boy, A Dog and Frog*, Phoenix
The Frog Princess, Coronet
Frog Went A-Courtin', Weston Woods

Books: *Seven Froggies Went to School*, Kate Duke
Periwinkle, Roger Duvoisin
Jump, Frog, Jump, Robert Kalan
The Mysterious Tadpole, Steven Kellogg
Better Move On, Frog!, Ron Maris

Fingerplay: Tadpoles. (Source: *Finger Frolics—Revised*, Liz Cromwell, Dixie Hibner, and John R. Faitel)

Craft: Egg Carton Frog. Construct a frog on a lily pad with the use of paint, paper, and cardboard egg cartons. These materials are easily available and easy for young children to handle. Items are generally available in the home for children to bring in.

This craft would require no more than one egg carton for each child. Add little paper legs. Flowers on the lily pad can be made from the cups of the egg carton and painted to add a bright touch. (Source: *Egg Carton Critters*, Donna Miller)

Activity: Leap Frog. Children love to pretend they are animals. This activity allows them great physical movements within the capabilities of children ages four and up. This game can also be played indoors and outdoors. (Source: *Games*, Anne Rockwell)

Song: "Froggie Went A'Courtin'" (Source: *The Fireside Book of Birds and Beasts*, Jane Yolen)

51 Ghosts

Filmstrips: *Georgie*, Weston Woods
The Ghost with the Halloween Hiccups, Random
House, Educational Enrichment Materials
The Legend of Sleepy Hollow, Walt Disney Educational
Media
Winnie the Witch and the Frightened Ghost, SVE

Books: *Bumps in the Night*, Harry Allard
A Ghost Named Fred, Nathaniel Benchley
Georgie and the Magician, Robert Bright
Babar and the Ghost, Laurent de Brunhoff
Gus Was a Friendly Ghost, Catherine Thayer

Fingerplay: Five Little Ghosts. (Source: *Finger Frolics—Revised*, Liz
Cromwell, Dixie Hibner, and John R. Faitel)

Craft: Ghost Friend. Make a ghost of your own that can stand on your
windowsill or as a centerpiece for your table. Napkins, a pencil, rubberband, and a cup are all that is required for this simple craft.
    To make it extra sweet try using a lollipop for the inside instead of a
pencil. (Source: *Beginning Crafts for Beginning Readers*, Alice Gilbreath)

Activity: A Lonely Little Ghost. Choose one child to be the lonely ghost.
Mark an area with tape on the floor for his home. The other children will try
to sneak into the area to tease the ghost while reciting a simple verse about
the ghost friend. (Text found on page 71 of the book.) Any child tagged will
become the ghost's friend and will help to catch the others. The last one
tagged wins the game. (Source: *New Games to Play*, Juel Krisvoy)

Song: "Casper, the Friendly Ghost" (Source: *The Reader's Digest
Children's Songbook*, Wiliam L. Simon)

52 Giants

Filmstrips: *Frog and Toad Together: Dragon and Giants*, Random
House
Jack and the Beanstalk, EBEC
Mickey and the Beanstalk, Walt Disney Educational
Media
Mickey Mouse, the Brave Little Tailor, Walt Disney
Educational Media
The Selfish Giant, Weston Woods

Films: *The Giant Devil-Dingo*, Weston Woods
The Selfish Giant, Weston Woods

Books: *Ribtickle Town*, Alan Benjamin
The Foolish Giant, Bruce Coville
Fin M'Coul, Tomie dePaola
The Pumpkin Giant, Ellin Greene
Giant John, Arnold Lobel

Fingerplay: The Giant and the Leprechaun. (Source: *Finger Frolics—
Revised*, Liz Cromwell, Dixie Hibner, and John R. Faitel)

Craft: Tin Can Stilts. Try to be a giant yourself by designing your own stilts
of tin cans and heavy cord. The exterior of the cans may be decorated to taste.
(Source: *Do a Zoom-Do*, Bernice Chesler)

Activity: Giant's Treasure. One child is chosen to be the sleeping giant who
lies guarding a pile of cookies and candies (or other treasures). While the
giant pretends to be asleep the other children attempt to steal the treasure.
When the giant sits up everyone freezes. Anyone caught moving is out of
the game. First to reach the treasure wins and becomes the next giant.
(Source: *500 Games*, Peter L. Cave)

53 Holidays: Chanukah

Filmstrips: *Hanukkah,* Britannica Learning Materials
Hanukkah Hot Cakes, SVE
The Story of Hanukkah and Christmas, SVE

Books: *A Picture Book of Hanukkah,* David Adler
Hanukkah Money, Sholom Aleichem
Laughing Latkes, M.B. Goffstein
I Love Hanukkah, Marilyn Hirsh
Potato Pancakes All Around, Marilyn Hirsh
The Odd Potato, Eileen Sherman

Rhyme: The Candle. (Source: *Finger Frolics—Revised,* Liz Cromwell, Dixie Hibner, and John R. Faitel)

Craft: Macaroni Star of David. Using lightweight cardboard, string, uncooked macaroni, gold spray paint, and other easily attainable items, a large star of David can be designed and hung as a mobile.

Select various types of macaroni and glue them to both sides of the cardboard star. When this is completed spray the entire thing with gold paint. This can be hung in the window for the holiday celebrations. This book contains many other suitable crafts. (Source: *Hanukkah Crafts,* Joyce Becker)

Activity: Chanukah Game. One player, Judah Maccabee, stands in his camp (a circle) while the other players (the Syrians) run in and out of the circle trying not to get tagged. Judah may not leave the camp, but the first player tagged must exchange places with him.

You may also find a delightful recipe for potato latkes in the source below to give the children a treat when the game is complete. (Source: *A Pumpkin in a Pear Tree,* Ann Cole, Carolyn Haas, Elizabeth Hellert, and Betty Weinberger)

Song: "My Dreydl" (Source: *The Holiday Song Book,* Robert Quackenbush)

54 Holidays: Christmas

Filmstrips: *Arthur's Christmas Cookies*, EBEC
                            The Bear Who Slept Through Christmas, SVE
                            The Boy Who Waited for Santa Claus, Random
                                    House, Educational Enrichment Materials
                            Lollipop Dragon Helps Santa, SVE
                            Morris' Disappearing Bag, Weston Woods

Films: *The Little Drummer Boy*, Weston Woods
                            The Mole and the Christmas Tree, Phoenix
                            The Twelve Days of Christmas, Weston Woods
                            A Visit from St. Nicholas, Coronet

Books: *Teddy's First Christmas*, Amanda Davidson
                            Petunia's Christmas, Roger Duvoisin
                            Claude the Dog, Dick Gackenbach
                            Katie and the Sad Noise, Ruth Gannett
                            Little Bear's Christmas, Janice

Fingerplay: Let's Build a Snowman. (Source: *Little Boy Blue*, Daphne Hogstrom)

Craft: Snowmobile. Winter snowmobiles can be constructed out of easily obtainable egg cartons. Painting and decorating of the snowmobiles can be left to available materials (crayons, paint, sticker, glitter, etc.). With construction paper or popsicle sticks you can add skis to the bottom.

The simple step-by-step instructions are illustrated. (Source: *Making Toys that Crawl and Slide*, Alice Gilbreath)

Activity: Christmas is Coming. This old English song includes a delightful dance that children may do. Props required here are pennies and an old hat. The children are only required to sit or skip while singing the short song while they place the penny in the old man's hat.

Actual sheet music is also provided. (Source: *Dancing Games for Children of all Ages*, Esther L. Nelson)

Song: "Jolly Old Saint Nicholas" (Source: *The Holiday Song Book*,
                            Robert Quackenbush)

55 Holidays: Easter

Filmstrips:	*The Bunnies' Easter Surprise*, SVE
	The Easter Basket Mystery, SVE
	Easter Bunnyland, Walt Disney Educational Media
	The King's Favorite Easter Egg Contest, Eye Gate Media
	Rackety Rabbit and the Runaway Easter Eggs, SVE
Film:	*The First Easter Rabbit*, Coronet
Books:	*The Easter Egg Artists*, Adrienne Adams
	Humbug Rabbit, Lorna Balian
	The Easter Bear, John Barrett
	The Funny Bunny Factory, Leonard Weisgard
	The Horse with the Easter Bonnet, Catherine Woolley

Fingerplay: Robbie the Rabbit. (Source: *Finger Frolics—Revised*, Liz Cromwell, Dixie Hibner, and John R. Faitel)

Craft: Easter Bunny Mobile. Little stand-up ears and whiskers that don't droop are featured on this smiling bunny face mobile constructed of paper plates. By putting the bunny face on both sides of the plate it can be hung as a mobile near a window or in a corner of the room. (Source: *Craft Fun*, Jane R. McCarty and Betty J. Peterson)

Activity: The Easter Bunny. This game and song allows the children to move around quickly using their entire bodies. While singing this delightful song they pretend to be rabbits thumping their feet, jumping, etc. (Source: *Singing Bee!: A Collection of Favorite Children's Songs*, Jane Hart)

Song:	"Peter Cottontail" or "The Bunny Hop" (Source: *The Reader's Digest Children's Songbook*, Wiliam L. Simon)

56 Holidays: Fourth of July

Filmstrips: *Holidays: Independence Day*, Random House
July Fourth and Summer Safety, Walt Disney
   Educational Media
Steven Kellogg's Yankee Doodle, Weston Woods
The Summer Snowman, Random House

Film: *Yankee Doodle*, Weston Woods

Books: *Henrietta's Fourth of July*, Syd Hoff
Festivals, Ruth Manning-Sanders
One Way: A Trip with Traffic Signs, Leonard Shortall
The Star Spangled Banner, Peter Spier
The Summer Snowman, Gene Zion

Fingerplay: The Flag. (Source: *Finger Frolics—Revised*, Liz Cromwell, Dixie Hibner, and John R. Faitel)

Craft: Firecracker Banks. Firecrackers are familiar items to children around this holiday. A safe firecracker that the children can use is a firecracker bank. These may be made using small cans, paint or construction paper coverings, and gold and red glitter pipe cleaners coming out of the lid. (Source: *Beginning Crafts for Beginning Readers*, Alice Gilbreath)

Activity: Happy Birthday USA. Small carnival-like games may be set up for the children to test their skills. Games may include: "Happy Birthday Ring Toss," "Uncle Sam's Fish Pond," and the "Liberty Bell Bean Bag Toss." (Source: *A Pumpkin in a Pear Tree*, Ann Cole, Carolyn Haas, Elizabeth Hellert, and Betty Weinberger)

Song: "Yankee Doodle" (Source: *Singing Bee!: A Collection of Favorite Children's Songs*, Jane Hart)

57 Holidays: Ground Hog's Day and Shadows

Filmstrips: *Christina and the Groundhog*, Clearvue
Groundhog's Day, SVE
Private Zoo, Live Oak Media

Film: *Tale of the Groundhog's Shadow*, Coronet

Books: *Wake Up, Groundhog!*, Carol Cohen
Groundhog's Day at the Doctor, Judy Delton
The Shadow Book, Beatrice deRegniers
Time for Jody, Wendy Kesselman
Nothing Sticks Like a Shadow, Ann Tompert

Fingerplay: Groundhog Day. (Source: *Rhymes for Learning Times*, Louise Binder Scott)

Craft: Silhouette Pictures. Tracing is something that many children practice a lot during the young years. Try having them trace shadows of plants, toy animals, or other still objects and then frame it to keep.

They may also try tracking their friends' shadows on the sidewalks with chalk. (Source: *Do a Zoom-Do*, Bernice Chesler)

Activity: Whose Little Shadow Are You? Each child has a partner who plays the shadow and must do whatever the first child does. After reciting and performing the acts stated, the child joins hands with his shadow and all race to see which pair reaches the door first. (Source: *New Games to Play*, Juel Krisvoy)

Song: "A Shadow and a Smile" (Source: *God's Wonderful World*, Agnes Leckie Mason and Phyllis Brown Ohanian)

58 Holidays: Halloween

Filmstrips: *Arthur's Halloween*, Random House
The Ghost with the Halloween Hiccups, Random
   House/Educational Enrichment Materials
Lollipop Dragon's First Halloween, SVE
Trick or Treat, Walt Disney Educational Media

Films: *Georgie*, Weston Woods
The Pumpkin Who Couldn't Smile, Coronet

Books: *Popcorn*, Frank Asch
Humbug Witch, Lorna Balian
Georgie's Halloween, Robert Bright
The Trip, Ezra Keats
Witch Bazooza, Dennis Nolan

Fingerplay: Halloween Surprise. (Source: *Finger Frolics—Revised*, Liz Cromwell, Dixie Hibner, and John R. Faitel)

Craft: Wanda Witch Puppet. Children enjoy puppets and having their own shows. Large Wanda, the Witch puppets can be made using paper plates, paper, and markers. This may be used as a puppet or as a mask held in front of the child's face. (Source: *Happy Halloween: Things to Make and Do*, Robyn Supraner)

Activity: Spider Web. Give each child a different color ball of string. At a signal each child will unwind the ball while wrapping it around a chair or some other specified object forming a spider web before the other children.
   Reverse it for the next game having the next child wind the ball back up. (Source: *A Pumpkin in a Pear Tree*, Ann Cole, Carolyn Haas, Elizabeth Hellert, and Betty Weinberger)

Song: "Have You See the Ghost of John?" (Source: *The Fireside Book of Children's Songs*, Marie Winn)

59 Holidays: St. Patrick's Day

(also includes Elves and Little People)

Filmstrips: *The Elves and the Shoemaker*, Britannica Learning
Materials
The Lavender Leprechaun, Walt Disney Educational
Media
Snow White and the 7 Dwarfs, Random House
St. Patrick's Day, SVE

Books: *Leprechauns Never Lie*, Lorna Balian
Little Bear Marches in the St. Patrick's Day Parade,
Janice Brustlein
The Hungry Leprechaun, Mary Calhoun
The Leprechaun's Story, Richard Kennedy
Daniel O'Rourke, Gerald McDermott

Fingerplay: The Giant and the Leprechaun. (Source: *Finger Frolics—
Revised*, Liz Cromwell, Dixie Hibner, and John R. Faitel)

Craft: Leprechaun's Clay Pipe. Although a clay pipe would be difficult and
time-consuming to make, how about one made of small drinking cups,
straws, and ribbons.

This book will give you short, simple instructions with an illustration for
making a Shillelagh and a leprechaun family. (Source: *Pin It, Tack It, Hang
It*, Phyllis and Noel Fiarotta)

Activity: Shamrock Hunt. Make several shamrocks with green construction paper. Put each child's name on a shamrock (if they can read their
names), and hide each in the room. Have each child try to find his or her
own. This can be played in teams with each team trying to find their names
first.

For those that can't read, put special pictures on the shamrocks for them
to locate. After the game, let the children make St. Patrick's Day hats and use
their shamrocks as a decoration at the top of each.

Song: "The Galway Piper" (Source: *The Rhythm Band Book*, Ruth
Etkin)

60 Holidays: St. Valentine's Day

Filmstrips: *Arthur's Valentine*, Random House
A Kiss for Little Bear, Weston Woods
Lollipop Dragon's Valentine Party, SVE
One Zillion Valentines, Random House
Raggedy Ann Learns a Lesson, SVE

Books: *The Great Valentine's Day Balloon Race*, Adrienne
Adams
The Valentine Bears, Eve Bunting
Bee My Valentine!, Miriam Cohen
The Hunt for Rabbit's Galosh, Ann Schweninger
The Best Valentine in the World, Marjorie Sharmat

Fingerplay: A Day for Love. (Source: *Finger Frolics—Revised*, Liz Cromwell, Dixie Hibner, and John R. Faitel)

Craft: Valentine Mobile. Allow the children to trace and cut out various size hearts for the mobile they will make. To add a touch of variety let them decorate the stars differently using stickers, crayon, and glitter.

Cut four strings of different lengths, and tape the hearts to these. Cut a wide strip of paper and staple it to form a circle. Each of the four strings of hearts can now be attached to this. Precut hearts could be used if time is short. (Source: *Let's Celebrate: Holiday Decorations You Can Make*, Peggy Parish)

Activity: Throne Game. The Queen of Hearts sit on her throne while the knave tries to steal a tart. The other guests stand on paper squares (the tarts). When the Queen says all change places, each guest tries to get to a new tart with the knave trying to steal one. If one is stolen, the person left out becomes the knave. (Source: *A Pumpkin in a Pear Tree*, Ann Cole, Carolyn Haas, Elizabeth Hellert, and Betty Weinberger)

Song: "Valentines" (Source: *God's Wonderful World*, Agnes Leckie Mason and Phyllis Brown Ohanian)

61 Holidays: Thanksgiving

Filmstrips: *Arthur's Thanksgiving*, Random House
The Bears Find Thanksgiving, SVE
The Boy Who Didn't Like Thanksgiving, Eye Gate Media
Indians for Thanksgiving, SVE
Thanksgiving in TumTum, SVE

Books: *Sometimes It's Turkey*, Lorna Balian
Thanksgiving Day, Gail Gibbons
Little Bear's Thanksgiving, Janice
One Tough Turkey, Steven Kroll
Thanksgiving at the Tappletons, Eileen Spinelli

Fingerplay: Five Little Turkeys. (Source: *Finger Frolics—Revised*, Liz Cromwell, Dixie Hibner, and John R. Faitel)

Craft: Paper Plate Turkey. There are many suggestions out there on how to make these brightly colored gobblers, and this is one of the easiest ones. Paper plates can be purchased rather cheaply and form the major part of the turkey with two glued to each other.

The tail feathers are created from looped construction paper. McCarty's book will even give you full-size patterns for making the feet and head so they look realistic.

A simple and enjoyable craft. (Source: *Craft Fun: Easy-to-Do with Simple Materials*, Janet R. McCarty and Betty J. Peterson)

Activity and Song: The Turkey Talk. While the children sing the song "Five Fat Turkeys Are We" they may take the parts of the turkey or the cooks. Piano music for the song is available for use in this source. Children enjoy depicting how animals will behave, and this dance will be enjoyed and asked for again and again. (Source: *Dancing Games for Children of All Ages*, Esther L. Nelson)

62 Hospitals/Doctors

Filmstrips: *Curious George Goes to the Hospital*, Random House, Educational Enrichment Materials
Lyle and the Birthday Party, Random House
Madeline, Random House
A Visit to the Hospital, SVE

Books: *Miffy in the Hospital*, Dick Bruna
A Visit to the Sesame Street Hospital, Deborah Hautzig
A Hospital Story, Sara Bonnett Stein
Emergency Mouse, Benard Stone
Betsy and the Doctor, Gunilla Wolde

Fingerplay: Five Little Monkeys. (Source: *Finger Frolics—Revised*, Liz Cromwell, Dixie Hibner, and John R. Faitel)

Craft and Activity: Stethoscope and Otoscope. Help the children learn about a doctor's instruments by constructing these familiar instruments from cups, paper and string. Later allow the children to practice with their paper instruments as you show real ones that you have obtained.

When children become familiar with these tools they will not become so frightened when they are used in the doctor's office.

This source also provides detailed instructions for making the following doctor's tools if you wish to extend this program into a full-unit lesson:

- Jar-of-Pills Signs
- Doctor's Bag
- Thermometer
- Hypodermic Syringe
- Blood Pressure Cuff
- Health Posters

These items can be simply and easily made out of construction paper and boxes. (Source: *Be What You Want to Be!*, Phyllis and Noel Fiarotta)

Song: "My Doctor" (Source: *God's Wonderful World*, Agnes Leckie Mason and Phyllis Brown Ohanian)

63 Houses/Homes

Filmstrips: *The Biggest House in the World*, Random House
The House on East 88th Street, Random House, Miller-
Brody
The Little House, Walt Disney Educational Media
Little Monster at Home, Listening Library
Oh, Were They Ever Happy, Listening Library

Film: *Grandfather's Mittens*, Phoenix

Books: *The Mouse in My House*, Catherine Chase
Where Does the Teacher Live?, Paula Feder
Pigs in the House, Steven Kroll
Better Move On, Frog!, Ron Maris
I Can Build a House!, Shigeo Watanabe

Fingerplay: My Home. (Source: *Finger Frolics—Revised*, Liz Cromwell, Dixie Hibner, and John R. Faitel)

Craft: A Doll House. A large cardboard carton can be transformed into a usable doll house. Leaving the flaps open, set the box on end and cut (or paint) windows in the front and sides. Dividers can be glued in to add a second floor.

The interior and exterior of the box can be painted to taste. Add a roof by folding posterboard in half and placing it on top. The interior can be designed by marker or by adding the children's toys. (Source: *Just a Box?*, Goldie Taub Chernoff)

Activity: Sweep the House. This is a simple team game that requires only the use of two brooms and two pieces of paper. Mark a circle at the center of the room and have the teams stand on opposite ends of the room. The goal is for each team member to try to sweep his garbage into the circle before his opponent. The team with the most winners wins the game. (Source: *New Games to Play*, Juel Krisvoy)

Song: "Home" (Source: *God's Wonderful World*, Agnes Leckie Mason and Phyllis Brown Ohanian)

64 Humor

Filmstrips: *Amelia Bedelia*, Random House
The Day Jimmy Boa Ate the Wash, Weston Woods
The Emperor's New Clothes, EBEC
Harold and the Purple Crayon, Weston Woods
Oh, The Thinks You Can Think, Random House

Films: *Caps for Sale*, Weston Woods
Pierre: A Cautionary Tale, Weston Woods
Rosie's Walk, Weston Woods

Books: *Miss Nelson Has a Field Day*, Harry Allard
Turtle Tale, Frank Asch
The Day the Teacher Went Bananas, James Howe
April Fools, Fernando Krahn
Too Much Noise, Ann McGovern

Fingerplay: Who Feels Happy Today? (Source: *Rhymes for Learning Times*, Louise Binder Scott)

Craft: Joke Box.

Monkey See, Monkey Do / Where's the monkey in the zoo?
Open the box and you will see / The only place the monkey can be.

Decorate a box using any available materials such as colored construction paper, stickers, markers. Allow the children to use their imagination. Inside glue a small mirror to the bottom of the box. Across the open section of the box bottom tape or glue black yarn to form a cage. Design and replace the box cover and you're set for a delightful joke with your friends.

Activity: I Saw a Purple Cow. This is a word game for two or more players. The first player says, "I saw a purple cow on the road. I ONE it." The next player says, "I TWO it" and so on until the eighth player says his line.

You can continue this game by changing the animals. It's lots of fun and no one loses. (Source: *I Saw a Purple Cow*, Ann Cole, Carolyn Haas, Faith Bushnell and Betty Weinberger)

Song: "A Bear Climbed Over the Mountain" (Source: *The Silly Songbook*, Esther L. Nelson)

65 Imagination and Pretending

Filmstrips: *The Emperor's New Clothes*, Britannica Learning
                Materials
             Harold and the Purple Crayon, Weston Woods
             McElligot's Pool, Random House
             My Friend from Outer Space, Random House, Educational
                Enrichment Materials
             Where the Wild Things Are, Weston Woods

Films: *In the Night Kitchen*, Weston Woods
             One Monday Morning, Weston Woods
             A Picture for Harold's Room, Weston Woods

Books: *Cloudy with a Chance of Meatballs*, Judi Barrett
             Quiet! There's a Canary in the Library, Don Freeman
             Harry and the Terrible Whatzit, Dick Gackenbach
             I Wish I Had Duck Feet, Theo LeSieg
             And to Think I Saw It on Mulberry Street, Dr. Seuss

Fingerplay: If. (Source: *Little Boy Blue*, Daphne Hogstrom)

Craft: Boogie Woogie Creatures. Have the children bring an old glove from home. With this give them each five medium size pom-poms of various colors to glue to the top of the glove's fingers. To each of these glue felt or craft store eyes. After they have dried the children may don the gloves and make the creatures dance to music by wiggling their fingers.

Activity: Let's Pretend We're Giants. This simple game requires the children to pretend they're giants. A rope is laid on the ground (rope river) and children must hop back and forth over it to reach the land of the little people. Those that step on the rope or fall have fallen into the river and are out of the game. (Source: *New Games to Play*, Juel Krisvoy)

Song: "I'm a Little Teapot" (Source: *Eye Winker, Tom Tinker, Chin Chopper*, Tom Glazer)

66 Insects

Filmstrips:	*Bootle Beetle*, Walt Disney Educational Media
	Charlie and the Caterpillar, EBEC
	A Fly Went By, Random House
	The Grasshopper and the Ants, Walt Disney Educational Media
	Sam and the Firefly, Random House
Films:	*The Ant and the Dove*, Coronet
	Why Mosquitoes Buzz in People's Ears, Weston Woods
Books:	*"I Can't," said the Ant*, Polly Cameron
	The Very Hungry Caterpillar, Eric Carle
	Never Say Ugh to a Bug, Norma Farber
	Ladybug, Ladybug, Fly Away Home, Judy Hawes
	Follow Me Cried Bee, Jan Wahl

Fingerplay: Roly-Poly Caterpillar. (Source: *Finger Frolics—Revised*, Liz Cromwell, Dixie Hibner, and John R. Faitel)

Craft: Clothespin Butterfly. A clothespin butterfly may be created using the following materials:

- Colored Paper
- Black Pipe Cleaners
- Clothespins (rounded tops)
- Crayons
- Stickers (dots of assorted colors)
- Patterns for wings

Children may trace and cut out the wings as one piece from the colored paper. This may be decorated as they wish using the dots and crayons provided. Pipe cleaners should be twisted around the top of the clothespin to form the antennae and the paper wings set between the prongs of the clothespin and fastened with tape.

Activity and Song: Eency Weency Spider. This book relates instructions for a fingerplay and dance to be done, besides including the words, written music, and a small record (45) of the music. (Source: *Dance-A-Folk Song*, Anne and Paul Barlin)

67 Kites

Suggestion: This may be related to a March Winds program.

Filmstrips: *Curious George Flies a Kite,* Random House
The Emperor and the Kite, Listening Library
The Kite Ride, SVE

Books: *Nu Dang and His Kite,* Jacqueline Ayer
Curious George Flies a Kite, Margaret Rey
Anatole Over Paris, Eve Titus
The Emperor and the Kite, Jane Yolen

Fingerplay: The Kite. (Source: *Finger Frolics—Revised,* Liz Cromwell, Dixie Hibner, and John R. Faitel)

Craft: Chinese Kite. This is a simple kite that may be constructed using a large, clear freezer bag. Distribute these to the children along with stickers and stars that they may put on the exterior of the bag. To make a tail for the kite, staple a length of colored ribbon to the unopened portion of the bag to give it balance. A small length of kite string taped to each side of the open section of the bag will allow it to fill up with air and open when the child runs with it.

With younger children (two years) you may wish to use a lunch bag instead of a freezer bag. Although it does give a different effect, some younger children may put the freezer bag over their heads if unattended. (Source: *More Beginning Crafts for Beginning Readers,* Alice Gilbreath)

Activity: Kite Run. The children should be escorted outdoors to demonstrate and play with their newly made kites. Whenever possible children should be given a chance to show off their creations, and this will give you an opportunity to demonstrate the correct way to use these kites.

Song: "Let's Go Fly a Kite" (Source: *The Walt Disney Song Book,* Walt Disney)

68 Libraries

Filmstrips: *Andy and the Lion*, Weston Woods
Check it Out, Listening Library
Finding What You Want (Lollipop Dragon), SVE
Library Manners for Primaries: Shh...Quiet Please, Eye
  Gate Media

Film: *Andy and the Lion*, Weston Woods

Books: *How My Library Grew*, Martha Alexander
Too Many Books!, Caroline Bauer
Quiet! There's a Canary in the Library, Don Freeman
A Visit to the Sesame Street Library, Deborah Hautzig
The Adventures of Cap'n O.G. Readmore, Fran
  Manushkin
Alistair in Outer Space, Marilyn Sadler

Fingerplay: I Wiggle. (Source: *Finger Frolics—Revised*, Liz Cromwell, Dixie
Hibner, and John R. Faitel)

Craft: Bookbug Bookmarks. A simple bookmark can be made by each
child as a momento of their library visit. They may be made using the
following materials: colored paper, crayons, large pom-poms, and small
eyes. Each child may decorate their precut bookmark as they wish. They
will then be given a pom-pom to glue on as the bookbug's head and then
eyes to glue on that.

Activity: A Walking Tour. A short walking of the library is essential in this
program. Such topics as the following should be covered:

- Location of books at the child's level
- Book care
- What's available at the library (besides books)
- Library manners

Note: A visit to the public library is suggested.

Song: "Member of the Library" (Source: *The Songs of Sesame Street
  in Poems and Pictures*, Jeffrey Moss, David Axelrod, Tony
  Geiss, Bruce Hart, Emily Perl Kingsley, and Jon Stone)

69 Magic

Filmstrips:	*Fat Magic*, EBEC
	Magic Fishbone, Listening Library
	The Magic Porridge Pot, Listening Library
	Rumplestiltskin, EBEC
Films:	*The Amazing Bone*, Weston Woods
	The Sorcerer's Apprentice, Weston Woods
	Strega Nonna, Weston Woods
Books:	*Humbug Potion*, Lorna Balian
	Georgie and the Magician, Robert Bright
	Big Anthony and the Magic Ring, Thomas dePaola
	The Frog Princess, Elizabeth Isele
	Sylvester and the Magic Pebble, William Steig

Craft: Magical Crystal Garden. The children will be delighted when they get to make their own crystal garden and watch it grow. Since a glass container is needed to grow the garden in you may want each child to bring in a small baby-food jar.

This will require such items as salt, water, laundry bluing, food coloring, charcoal, and ammonia (do not leave children unsupervised during this since ammonia is used). For actual proportions, check in the book listed here. (Source: *Craft Fun: Easy to Do Projects with Simple Materials*, Janet R. McCarty and Betty J. Peterson)

Activity: The Magic Feather. This game is essentially to develop body awareness and relaxation. While the children sit in a circle with their eyes closed someone touches them with the magic feather. The child must, with eyes still closed, touch the same part of the body that was touched by the feather. If he succeeds he may get to use the feather next. (Source: *Teacher's Handbook of Children's Games*, Marian Jenks Wirth)

Song:	"Puff the Magic Dragon" (Source: *The Reader's Digest Children's Songbook*, Wiliam L. Simon)

70 Manners and Etiquette

Filmstrips: *The Circus Baby*, Weston Woods
        Thank You, Amelia Bedelia, Random House
        What Do You Do, Dear?, Weston Woods
        What Do You Say, Dear?, Weston Woods

Film: *The Selfish Giant*, Weston Woods

Books: *Perfect Pig*, Marc Brown
        Periwinkle, Roger Duvoisin
        Dinner at Alberta's, Russell Hoban
        Mind Your Manners, Peggy Parish
        Richard Scarry's Please and Thank You Book, Richard
            Scarry

Fingerplay: Sometimes My Hands Are Naughty. (Source: *Finger Frolics—Revised*, Liz Cromwell, Dixie Hibner, and John R. Faitel)

Craft: Helping Hands. Have each child make a paint print of their hands to be framed and labeled "__(name)__'s HELPING HANDS." Have all the children recite the following pledge and present the hands to their parents:

> "I promise to help friends whenever I can and to remember to say thank you when someone helps me."

Activity: Mother, May I?. This game is one that is familiar to most children. The leader may be another child or the teacher. The children begin at one end of the room and try to reach the leader by taking the amount of steps that the leader says they may take. The child must first remember to say "Mother, may I?" before taking those steps or he will have to return to the beginning of the course. The child who reaches the leader first becomes the new leader.

Song: "A Child's Prayer of Thanks" (Source: *God's Wonderful World*, Agnes Leckie Mason and Phyllis Brown Ohanian)

71 Mixed-Up Creatures

Filmstrips: *The Lorax*, Random House
McElligot's Pool, Random House
Professor Wormbog in the Search for the Zimper-a-zoo,
 Listening Library
The Sneetches, Random House
The Story of the Little Mermaid, EBEC

Film: *The Zax*, Phoenix

Books: *Cynthia and the Unicorn*, Jean Freeman
Hansy's Mermaid, Trinka Noble
I Wish I Had Duck Feet, Theo LeSieg
The Bunyip of Berkeley's Creek, Jenny Wagner

Fingerplay: The Centaur. (Source: *Finger Frolics—Revised*, Liz Cromwell, Dixie Hibner, and John R. Faitel)

Craft: Imaginary Creatures. With the popularity of the Wuzzles, a simple mix-up of animals' parts can make a popular craft. Cut up illustrations of different types of animals and allow the children to mix and match the parts to create their own characters.

When they've selected the parts they want to match help them mount them on large construction paper. They can then color them if needed or leave them as they are. Ask each child to identify what animal each part really belongs to.

Activity: The Hopfly Bird. A small verse in this game describes the hopfly bird as a bird that must hop high to be able to fly.

Make a mark high on the wall that the children cannot reach by standing but may be able to reach by hopping high. The children line up to pretend to be hopfly birds. They each get to hop three times to try to reach the spot. The child who reaches it in the least amount of hops is the winner and is the best hopfly bird.

Children may later attempt to imitate other mixed up animals by having their actions and voices do different things. (E.g., a frog that meows—hop like a frog while meowing like a cat.) (Source: *New Games to Play*, Juel Krisvoy)

Song: "The Lion and the Unicorn" (Source: *Sing Hey Diddle Diddle*, Beatrice Harrop)

72 Monsters

Filmstrips: *Andrew and the Strawberry Monsters*, EBEC
Monster Seeds, EBEC
Monsters in the Closet, EBEC
There's a Nightmare in my Closet, Listening Library
Where the Wild Things Are, Weston Woods

Film: *Leopold the See-Through Crumbpicker*, Weston Woods

Books: *Harry (the monster)*, Ann Cameron
The Marigold Monster, M.C. Delaney
Annie and the Mud Monster, Dick Gackenbach
Love from, Aunt Betty, Nancy Parker
I Was a Second Grade Werewolf, Daniel Pinkwater

Fingerplay: Five Little Monsters. (Source: *Finger Frolics—Revised*, Liz Cromwell, Dixie Hibner, and John R. Faitel)

Craft: Egg Carton Creature. Begin with the bottom of an egg carton turned upside down. Add a string to the face of the creature to pull it along. The child may use paper to put on legs, wings, etc. as desired. A beautiful illustration sample is available in the source below. (Source: *Lollipop, Grapes and Clothespin Critters: Quick, On-the-Spot Remedies for Restless Children 2-10*, Robyn Freedman Spizman)

Activity: Costume Party. Have a "Worst Monster Competition." Allow the children to come dressed as a scary or humorous monster. Let them parade for the group to any eerie music available and award paper ribbons in various categories. (Suggestion: At this age all should get some type of award.)

Song: "The Ghost of John" (Source: *Rounds About Rounds*, Jane Yolen)

73 Music and Musical Instruments

Filmstrips: *The Birthday Trombone,* EBEC
The Bremen-Town Musicians, Random House
Emil, the Tap-Dancing Frog, EBEC
The Foolish Frog, Weston Woods
I Know an Old Lady Who Swallowed a Fly,
Listening Library

Films: *Frog Went A-Courtin',* Weston Woods
Lentil, Weston Woods
Really Rosie, Weston Woods

Books: *Mama Don't Allow,* Thatcher Hurd
Ben's Trumpet, Rachel Isadora
Geraldine, the Music Mouse, Leo Lionni
Really Rosie, Maurice Sendak
Anatole and the Piano, Eve Titus

Fingerplay: If I Could Play. (Source: *Finger Frolics—Revised,* Liz Cromwell, Dixie Hibner, and John R. Faitel)

Craft: Musical Band. Create your own musical instruments including a tissue box ukelele, a musical comb humdinger, maracas, a one-string bass fiddle, a straw tooter, or cymbal crashers from simple, easily accessible supplies.

Follow the simple directions given on page 24-29 of McCarty and Peterson's book, and your group can create their own band. Instructions are accompanied by a clear set of illustrations to follow. (Source: *Craft Fun: Easy-to-do Projects with Simple Materials,* Janet R. McCarty and Betty J. Peterson)

Activity: Bash and Bang Band. This is a parading song and activity to allow the children to use their newly made instruments or to just pretend they have their favorite instruments. Sheet music is made available on a two-page spread. This song will also allow the children to call out and identify their particular instruments. (Source: *Game-Songs with Prof Dogg's Troupe,* Harriet Powell)

Song: "Brother, Come and Dance with Me" (Source: *Eye Winker, Tom Tinker, Chin Chopper,* Tom Glazer)

74 Names

Filmstrips: *The Boy Who Would Not Say His Name,* Random
House, Educational Enrichment Materials
Hooper Humperdink..? Not Him!, Random House
Rumplestiltskin, EBEC
Tikki-Tikki-Tembo, Weston Woods

Books: *Sabrina,* Martha Alexander
The Other Emily, Gibbs Davis
Andy (that's my name), Tomi dePaola
Wind Rose, Crescent Dragonwagon
But Names Will Never Hurt Me, Bernard Waber

Fingerplay: Two Little Dickybirds. (Source: *Little Boy Blue,* Daphne
Hogstrom)

Craft: Nameplates. Make your own special nameplates to be hung on the
bedroom door, your toybox, or on other special places. Four methods are
described in the source cited. For those children who still don't recognize
their name, have it written on a card for them to copy or make the letters
available by having them already cut out of magazines. (Source: *Purple Cow
to the Rescue,* Ann Cole, Carolyn Haas, and Betty Weinberger)

Activity: New-Neighbor Games. Trade a name allows each child to print
his name on many strips of paper. The children may trade their strips with
their newly made friends and create a friendship chain with these strips.
They should try to get one strip from everyone in the room by trading off one
of theirs. They should be sure to keep trading until they are sure they don't
have any duplicate names in their possession. The first to do this is the
winner.
They can then chain them together with glue or tape to create their own
chain friendship belt.

Song: "Bingo" (Source: *Reader's Digest Children's Songbook,* William
L. Simon)

75 Noise/Sounds

Filmstrips: *Bears in the Night*, Random House
Goodnight, Owl!, Weston Woods
Harry and the Lady Next Door, Random House, Miller-
    Brody
Lentil, Weston Woods
Noisy Nora, Weston Woods

Books: *Bumps in the Night*, Harry Allard
Petunia and the Song, Roger Duvoisin
Katie and the Sad Noise, Ruth Gannett
Shhhh!, Suzy Kline
Too Much Noise!, Ann McGovern

Fingerplay: Tap and Clap. (Source: *Children's Counting-Out Rhymes, Fingerplays, Jump-Rope and Bounce-Ball Chants and Other Rhythms,* Gloria T. Delamar)

Craft and Activity: Maraca Rhythm Maker. Music can be made by the simple use of tongue depressors, beans or macaroni, and small paper cups. Have the children create their own maracas.

Also have other rhythm instruments available for the children to experiment with. Simple lessons in rhythm using these instruments will be enjoyed by all. (Source: *Craft Fun: Easy-to-Do Projects with Simple Materials,* Janet R. McCarty and Betty J. Peterson)

Song: "Listen to the Noises" (Source: *Music for Ones and Twos,* Tom
    Glazer)

76 Old Age

Filmstrips: *The Bremen Town Musicians*, Random House
Cloudy with a Chance of Meatballs, Live Oak Media
I Know an Old Lady Who Swallowed a Fly, Listening
   Library
Old Blue, EBEC
Old Mother Hubbard and Her Dog, Weston Woods

Books: *It's So Nice to Have a Wolf Around the House*, Harry
   Allard
Fish for Supper, M.B. Goffstein
The Snow Child, Freya Littledale
Mrs. Periwinkle's Groceries, Pegeen Snow
Could Be Worse!, James Stevenson

Fingerplay: Grandma. (Source: *Finger Frolics—Revised*, Liz Cromwell, Dixie Hibner, and John R. Faitel)

Craft: The Old Woman in the Shoe. Make the old woman's shoe home using construction paper, crayons, and tape or staples. A child's conception of the old woman's shoe may vary with what they think the shoe should look like. Patterns of various types of shoes can be made available for tracing. After completion of the craft, show the children the illustrations of this story.

Activity: This Old Man. Children may act out this song in any number of ways:

- act out the numbers by holding up fingers
- act out objects mentioned
- clap the rhythm of the song or
- use instruments to beat out the measure

(Source: *Teacher's Handbook of Children's Games*, Marian Jenks Wirth)

Song: "Grandma's Spectacles" (Source: *Eye Winker, Tom Tinker, Chin Chopper*, Tom Glazer)

77 Pets

Filmstrips:	*The Biggest Bear*, Weston Woods
	Harry the Dirty Dog, Random House
	Pet Stories: Bassetts Aren't People, EBEC
	Pet Stories: The Hamsters Who Hid, EBEC
	Pet Stories: The Parakeet Who Panicked, EBEC

Film: *The Mysterious Tadpole*, Weston Woods

Books:	*No Ducks in Our Bathtub*, Martha Alexander
	The Great Hamster Hunt, Lenore Blegvad
	The Habits of Rabbits, Virginia Kahl
	Pet Show!, Ezra Keats
	Positively No Pets Allowed, Nathan Zimelman

Fingerplay: A Kitten. (Source: *Finger Frolics—Revised*, Liz Cromwell, Dixie Hibner, and John R. Faitel)

Craft: Kitten Bank. A small cardboard box can be transferred into a delightful cat bank with whiskers and all. The suggested box is the small type (tissue box, oatmeal box, etc.). With construction paper you can make a head and tail to add to the box ends. Use pipe cleaners for whiskers. Paint the box itself to match the color of the head. Cut a small opening for the money. (Source: *Highlights Magazine for Children*, Barbara Bell, ed., April, 1984)

Activity: A 4-H Pet Show. Invite your local 4-H group to bring their pets to the program and speak to the children about these animals. These pets may include hamsters, rabbits, ducks, etc. This will allow small children an opportunity to see and touch animals they may have never touched before.

Song: "I Love Little Pussy" (Source: *Songs and Rhymes for Little Children*, no author)

78 Plants/Seeds

Filmstrips: *Frog and Toad Together: The Garden*, Random House
Jack and the Beanstalk, EBEC
Mickey and the Beanstalk, Walt Disney Educational
    Media
Monster Seeds, EBEC
The Turnip, MacMillan

Film: *The Little Red Hen*, Coronet

Books: *The Tiny Seed*, Eric Carle
The Marigold Monster, M.C. Delaney
The Carrot Seed, Ruth Krauss
The Remarkable Plant in Apt. 4, Giulio Maestro
The Plant Sitter, Gene Zion

Fingerplay: My Garden. (Source: *Finger Frolics—Revised*, Liz Cromwell, Dixie Hibner, and John R. Faitel)

Craft: Berry Basket Planter. Using plastic berry baskets saved from stores, the children may weave a beautiful basket with colorful ribbon. Seeds may be planted within and a paper flower made and placed in the dirt temporarily until the children's real flowers grow. Simple scraps can be made into a craft the children will take pride in. (Source: *Scrapcraft: 50 Easy to Make Handicraft Projects*, Judith Choate and Jane Green)

Activity: Growing Flowers. Calming music may be played while allowing the children to pretend they are seeds all curled up. As the teacher circulates around the room, the child that's touched on the head pretends to grow into a type of flower he or she likes best.
    Later have the children tell what kind of flower they are and how it feels to grow like a flower.

Song: "I Had a Little Nut Tree" (Source: *Sing Hey Diddle Diddle*, Beatrice Harrop)

79 Poetry

Filmstrips: *The Bear Detectives*, Random House
               Horton Hatches an Egg, Random House
               I'll Teach My Dog 100 Words, Random House
               Madeline's Rescue, Weston Woods
               Put Me in the Zoo, Random House

Films: *Madeline*, LCA
               Owl and the Pussycat, Weston Woods

Books: *Who Sank the Boat?*, Pamela Allen
               Ten, Nine, Eight, Molly Bang
               Frances Face-Maker, William Cole
               Roll Over!, Mordicai Gerstein
               Who Wants a Cheap Rhinoceros?, Shel Silverstein

Fingerplay: Wee Willie Winkle. (Source: *Children's Counting-Out Rhymes, Fingerplays, Jump-Rope and Bounce-Ball Chants and Other Rhythms*, Gloria T. Delamar)

Craft and Activity: Monster Poetry. Children enjoy monsters, as long as they're not too scary. Distribute materials such as construction paper, crayons, sticker dots, feathers, etc. for children to create their own monsters. Attach the creation to a stick, and it may become a puppet easily handled.

Place the monster in a box and have the children bring it out at the end of this old folk rhyme, "In a Dark, Dark Wood." The words for this rhyme can also be found in the book, *A Dark, Dark Tale* by Ruth Brow. (Source: *This Way to Books*, Caroline Feller Bauer)

Song: "I'm Being Eaten By a Boa Constrictor" (Source: *The Silly Songbook*, Esther L. Nelson)

80 Reptiles: Alligators, Crocodiles

Filmstrips: *Alligators All Around*, Weston Woods
Alligators Are Awful, Spoken Arts
Crocus, Random House
Frederick's Alligator, EBEC
Lyle, Lyle Crocodile, Random House

Jerome the Babysitter, Eileen Christelow
Alligator's Toothache, Diane DeGroat
Dinner at Alberta's, Russell Hoban
There's a Crocodile Under My Bed!, Ingrid
    Schubert
Millicent Maybe, Ellen Weiss

Fingerplay and Song: The Crocodile. (Source: *Do Your Ears Hang Low?*,
Tom Glazer)

Craft: Egg Carton Crocodile. Make a crocodile puppet that's easy to work
out of everyday egg cartons. The lower half of an egg carton may even be
turned upside down in the puppet's mouth to form the crocodile's teeth. If
you want to make the crocodile longer and, at the same time, hide your arm,
attach a long piece of green cloth to the egg carton heads. (Source: *Egg
Carton Critters*, Donna Miller)

Activity: Crocodile Hunt. One child sits on the floor in the center of the
room in the middle of a circle. This child crawls along the floor within the
circle (lake) as a crocodile would move. He suddenly stands up, rising from
the water, to spot his victim. Other children circulate through the room.
When the crocodile rises all must freeze. Those who still move are captured
by the crocodile and are out of the game. (Source: *500 Games*, Peter L. Cave)

81 Reptiles: Snakes

Filmstrips: *The Birthday Trombone*, EBEC
Crictor, Weston Woods
The Day Jimmy's Boa Ate the Wash, Weston Woods
Snakes, Clearvue

Film: *The Boy and the Boa*, Phoenix

Books: *Snake In, Snake Out*, Linda Banchek
Joseph and the Snake, Howard Berson
Slithers, Syd Hoff
Jimmy's Boa Bounces Back, Trinka Noble
Mrs. Peloki's Snake, Joanne Oppenheim

Fingerplay: The Snake. (Source: *Games for the Very Young*, Elizabeth Matterson)

Craft: Snake. Construct a brightly colored snake with numerous colored felt, scissors, and glue. Simply cut a long strip for the body and small oval shapes to fill it out. Don't forget the tongue. (Source: *Do a Zoom-Do*, Bernice Chesler)

Activity: Snake by the Tail. This may be played outdoors or indoors in a large room. All players line up behind each other holding their hands on the waist of the person before them. The leader must try to touch the snake's tail (last person) taking everyone else with him. Anyone who breaks the chain is out. If the leader succeeds, he goes to the end of the snake and the new leader takes his place at the head. (Source: *500 Games*, Peter L. Cave)

Song: "I'm Being Eaten By a Boa Constrictor" (Source: *The Silly Songbook*, Esther L. Nelson)

82 Reptiles: Turtles

Filmstrips: *The Fractured Turtle,* Imperial Film Company
Pluto's Surprise Package, Walt Disney Educational
Media
The Tortoise and the Hare, Walt Disney Educational
Media
Yertle the Turtle, Random House

Books: *Turtle Tale,* Frank Asch
Timothy Turtle, Al Graham
Turtle Spring, Lillian Hoban
Harry and Shelburt, Dorothy VanWoerkom
Albert's Toothache, Barbara Williams

Fingerplay and Song: I Had a Little Turtle. (Source: *Reaching the Special Learner Through Music,* no author)

Craft: Paper Turtle. Using the large format shown in this book, which is appropriate for the manual dexterity of this age, children can color and glue together the parts of a turtle. Large pieces make it easy for the children to handle the work they're doing. The illustrations in this book can be easily duplicated for use. (Source: *Big and Easy Art,* Teacher Created Materials, Inc.)

Activity: Great Turtle Race. The turtles constructed in the previous craft described may be attached to a string going through a hole. Attach one end of the string to a stationary object, while the child holds the other end parallel to the floor. The player should then ease up on the string and quickly pull it tight again. This continuous motion will move the turtle to the opposite end of the string. (Source: *Steven Caney's Toy Book,* Steven Caney)

83 Royalty

Filmstrips:	*Babar Loses His Crown,* Random House
	Cinderella, Walt Disney Educational Media
	The Emperor's New Clothes, Britannica Learning Materials
	The King, the Mice and the Cheese, Random House
	The Story of King Midas, EBEC
Films:	*The Most Wonderful Egg in the World,* Weston Woods
	One Monday Morning, Weston Woods
	Many Moons, McGraw
Books:	*The Princess and the Pea,* H.C. Andersen
	The Frog Prince, Jane Canfield
	Rumplestiltskin, Jacob Grimm
	King Henry's Palace, Pat Hutchins
	The Practical Princess, Jay Williams

Fingerplay: Sing a Song of Sixpence. (Source: *Finger Frolics—Revised,* Liz Cromwell, Dixie Hibner, and John R. Faitel)

Craft: King's Crown. A regal king's crown can be constructed with nothing more than construction paper and staples or tape. A band of paper the circumference of the child's head can be cut. Strips of an alternate color can be folded in loops and attached all around the band. More suggestions for decorating the band and making a queen's crown can be found in the book listed here. (Source: *Rainy Day Magic,* Margaret Perry)

Activity: Throne Game. The Queen of Hearts sits on her throne while the knave tries to steal a tart. The other guests stand on paper squares (the tarts). When the Queen says all change places, each guest tries to get to a new tart with the knave trying to steal one. If one is stolen, the person left out becomes the knave. (Source: *A Pumpkin in a Pear Tree,* Ann Cole, Carolyn Haas, Elizabeth Hellert, and Betty Weinberger)

Song:	"Old King Cole" (Source: *Singing Bee!: A Collection of Favorite Children's Songs,* Jane Hart)

84   Safety

Filmstrips: *The Bear's Vacation,* Random House
Bicycle Safety: Safety on Wheels with Goofy,
Walt Disney Educational Media
I'm No Fool with Fire, Walt Disney Educational Media
I'm No Fool with Poisons, Walt Disney Educational
Media
*Winnie the Pooh on the Way to School: Tigger Becomes
a Pedestrian,* Walt Disney Educational Media

Film: *Meeting Strangers: Red Light, Green Light,* Phoenix

Books: *The Bike Lesson,* Stan and Jan Berenstain
Red Light! Green Light!, Margaret Wise Brown
Matches, Lighters and Firecrackers Are Not Toys, Dorothy Chlad
No! No!, Lois Myller
Try It Again, Sam, Judith Viorst

Fingerplay: At the Curb. (Source: *Finger Frolics—Revised,* Liz Cromwell,
Dixie Hibner, and John R. Faitel)

Craft: The Traffic Light. The source below gives a page to duplicate a traffic
light on strong poster board. Have the children fill in the proper colors. By
putting the colors on removable strips this can be used for traffic games
later.
   Place it on your bedroom door to indicate whether or not you want
people to come in. (Source: *101 Easy Art Activities,* Trudy Aarons and
Francine Koelsch)

Activity: Red Light, Green Light. Children must run slowly on the word
'green,' walk on 'yellow,' and freeze on 'red.' A tom-tom can be used to
indicate the type of motion, too. This game develops the ability to stop and
start with quick reactions. (Source: *Teacher's Handbook of Children's Games,*
Marian Jenks Wirth)

Song: "The Traffic Cop" (Source: *This is Music,* William R. Sur, Mary
R. Tolbert, William R. Fisher, and Adeline McCall)

85 Sea and Seashore

Filmstrips: *The Bear's Vacation*, Random House
Harry By the Sea, Random House, Miller-Brody
I'm No Fool in Water, Walt Disney Educational Media
Little Tim and the Brave Sea Captain, Weston Woods

Books: *Sand Cake*, Frank Asch
The Seashore Noisy Book, Margaret Wise Brown
Teddy at the Seashore, Amanda Davidson
Starfish, Edith Hurd
I Was All Thumbs, Benard Waber

Fingerplay: Five Little Seashells. (Source: *Finger Frolics—Revised*, Liz Cromwell, Dixie Hibner, and John R. Faitel)

Craft: Shell Necklace or Belt. With a collection of small shells and some kite string, children can make their own necklaces or belts. Holes in the shells should be done before the program. The shells may be left natural or painted if time permits.

Activity: Fishing. Set up a small child's pool in the room (no water, please). Inside have numerous small paper fish with small metal tabs glued near the mouth portion. Give each child a small fishing pole (string and stick with a magnet on it) and have them catch as many fish as they can in a given period of time.

Song: "She Waded in the Water" (Source: *Do Your Ears Hang Low?*, Tom Glazer)

86 Seasons: Fall

Filmstrips: *Autumn*, Educational Activities Inc.
Let's Find Out About Fall, Random House
Winnie the Pooh and the Blustery Day, Walt Disney
Educational Media
*Winnie the Pooh Discovers the Seasons: Pooh and Owl
Have a Fall Adventure*, Walt Disney Educational
Media

Books: *All Ready for School*, Leone Adelson
Now It's Fall, Lois Lenski
Henry Explores the Mountains, Mark Taylor
Emily's Autumn, Janice Udry
Marmalade's Yellow Leaf, Cindy Wheeler

Fingerplay: Leaves Are Floating Down. (Source: *Finger Frolics—Revised*,
Liz Cromwell, Dixie Hibner, and John R. Faitel)

Craft: Nature Mobile. While the children are outside for the fall activity
games have them collect leaves, pine cones, seed pods, etc. from the area.
With these items, string, and a hanger a simple mobile may be created.
(Source: *Something to Make, Something to Think About*, Martha Olson Condit)

Activity: Sparrows and Statues. A game similar to the well-known 'Freeze
Tag,' children pretend to be sparrows hopping and flying around until the
caller yells stop, then all must freeze in position. Those who do not freeze
are out of the game. Prizes may be given for the funniest poses. (Source: *500
Games*, Peter L. Cave)

Song: "Pretty Leaves" (Source: *God's Wonderful World*, Agnes
Leckie Mason and Phyllis Brown Ohanian)

87   Seasons: Spring

Filmstrips: *Frog and Toad Are Friends: Spring*, Random
House, Miller-Brody
Let's Find Out About Spring, Random House
Springtime for Jeanne-Marie, Random House, Miller-
Brody
*Winnie the Pooh Discovers the Seasons: Pooh Catches
Spring Fever*, Walt Disney Educational Media

Film: *Ladybug, Ladybug, Winter Is Coming!*, Coronet

Books: *One Bright Monday Morning*, Arline Baum
Wake Up, Groundhog!, Carlo Cohen
Sleepy Bear, Lydia Dabcovich
Little Bear's Pancake Party, Janice
Really Spring, Gene Zion

Fingerplay: Little Brown Seed. (Source: *Finger Frolics—Revised*, Liz
Cromwell, Dixie Hibner, and John R. Faitel)

Craft: Paper Flowers. With the use of paper, straws, glue, scissors, and a
coffee can children will be guided in making a small flower garden of their
own.
   Try showing the children pictures of various types of flowers so they can
have variety in their design. The most popular and easiest of designs is the
tulip or the daisy. Precut patterns for the children to trace will save time and
frustration for this age level. (Source: *Fun with Paper*, Robyn Supraner)

Activity: The Farmer and His Seeds. The following activity may be performed while singing the words to the tune "Farmer in the Dell."

The Farmer plants the seeds
The Farmer plants the seeds
Hi, Ho, the dairy-o
The Farmer plants the seeds   (bend and pretend to plant)

The sun comes out to shine, etc. (make circle with arms)
The rain begins to fall, etc. (fingers flutter up and down)
The plant begins to grow, etc. (slowly raise up)
The farmer cuts them down, etc. (cutting motion)
And now he grinds it up, etc. (grinding motion)
And now he bakes the bread, etc. (put in oven)
And now we'll have some bread. (pretend to eat)

Activity and Song: Over in the Meadow. This includes instructions for a short dance, as well as, music and lyrics to a song which will help the children identify animals and insects appearing in the spring. (Source: *Dancing Games for Children of All Ages*, Esther L. Nelson)

88 Seasons: Summer

Filmstrips: *The Bear's Vacation*, Random House
Frog and Toad Are Friends: A Swim, Random House, Miller-Brody
July Fourth and Summer Safety, Walt Disney Educational Media
Summer, Random House
The Summer Snowman, Random House

Books: *The Swimming Hole*, Jerrold Beim
The Berenstain Bears Go to Camp, Stan Berenstain
The Summer Noisy Book, Margaret Wise Brown
Harry by the Sea, Gene Zion
Summer Is..., Charlotte Zolotow

Fingerplay: The Rain. (Source: *Finger Frolics—Revised*, Liz Cromwell, Dixie Hibner, and John R. Faitel)

Craft: Matchbox Boat. A simple boat of paper, sticks, foil, clay, and paint can be constructed in minutes. This craft requires minimal skills and provides immediate rewards. Five-step illustrated instructions can be located in Ms. Pitcher's book.

REMEMBER: Have a tub available to allow the children to test out their creations. Immediate reward is helpful at this age.

(Source: *Cars and Boats*, Caroline Pitcher)

Activity: Magnet Fishing. This takes a bit of preparation beforehand. It will require a small tub or swimming pool, paper fish cut with metal tabs on them, and sticks with string and magnets at the end.

The game can be played in a number of ways:

- Place number scores on certain fish to allow the children to try to get the highest score by catching fish with the high numbers.
- Have certain children try to catch designated colored fish. The first to collect all his color wins.

(Source: *500 Games*, Peter L. Cave)

Song: "Row, Row, Row Your Boat" (Source: *Rounds and Rounds*, Jane Yolen)

89 Seasons: Winter

Filmstrips: *The Big Snow*, Weston Woods
Henry the Explorer, Weston Woods
Josie and the Snow, Weston Woods
Snow, Random House

Film: *The Snowy Day*, Weston Woods

Books: *Winter Noisy Book*, Margaret Wise Brown
Katy and the Big Snow, Virginia Burton
Where Does Everyone Go?, Aileen Fisher
Old Turtle's Winter Games, Leonard Kessler
Frederick, Leo Lionni

Fingerplay: Snowflakes. (Source: *Finger Frolics—Revised*, Liz Cromwell, Dixie Hibner, and John R. Faitel)

Craft: Paper Plate Penguins. Construct a penguin of paper plates and construction paper. Precut parts are advisable for this craft. Two sizes of plates are needed for each child, a six-inch cake plate for the head and a nine-inch plate for the body. This book gives you true-to-size patterns to trace for the eyes, feet, head, beak, and wings of the penguin. (Source: *Paper Plate Animals*, Bee Gee Hazell)
    or
Snow Scene: Make a simple winter scene. Give each child a sheet of black or blue construction paper. Have them cut three different sizes of white circles to glue on to form a snowman. (Precut circles for two- or three-year-olds is advisable.) Use real material of various colors for the scarf and hat. Use chalk to draw the snow on the ground and small, white sticker dots for the snow falling from the sky. Stickers are a popular item in crafts at a young age.

Activity and Song: "Shovel the Snow". Allow the children to act out the motions of shoveling snow when this is sung in the song.
    Try adapting the song to add other verses of what you can do with snow. (Source: *God's Wonderful World*, Agnes Leckie Mason and Phyllis Brown Ohanian)

90 Space and Spaceships

Filmstrips: *Curious George Gets a Medal*, Random House, Educational
        Enrichment Materials
        Earth Day and the Galaxy Gnomes, Clearvue
        My Friend from Outer Space, Random House, Educational
        Enrichment Materials

Film: *Many Moons*, Rembrandt Films

Books: *Harold's Trip to the Sky*, Crockett Johnson
        Regards to the Man in the Moon, Ezra Keats
        What Next, Baby Bear!, Jill Murphy
        Alistair in Outer Space, Marilyn Sadler
        Pigs in Space, Ellen Weiss

Fingerplay: Ten Little Martians. (Source: *Finger Frolics—Revised*, Liz Cromwell, Dixie Hibner, and John R. Faitel)

Craft: A UFO You Can Fly. A paper-plate flying saucer may be decorated simply using plates, glue, crayons, and a little imagination. A chance to use these UFO's outside would be welcomed by young children.
  Mr. Ross' entire book is devoted to showing young children how to make at least eight different types of UFO's out of inexpensive materials. (Source: *Making UFO's*, Dave Ross)
  or
  A Felt Space Picture. Using a square of dark felt for the sky, some varied colored felt to cut out spaceships, a pole and string, a delightful banner can be designed. This is an uncomplicated banner that young preschoolers can handle. An illustration is available. (Source: *Felt Craft*, Florence Temko)

Activity and Song: One Little, Two Little, Three Little Spacemen. (Source: *I Saw a Purple Cow and 100 Other Recipes for Learning* Ann Cole, Carolyn Haas, Faith Bushnell, and Betty Weinberger)

91 Sports

Filmstrips: *Frog and Toad Are Friends: A Swim,* Random
House, Miller-Brody
McElligot's Pool, Random House
Play Ball, Amelia Bedelia, Random House
The Tortoise and the Hare, Walt Disney Educational
Media

Books: *Arthur Goes to Camp,* Marc Brown
The Littlest Leaguer, Syd Hoff
Wait, Skates!, Mildred Johnson
Kick, Pass and Run, Leonard Kessler
Gone Fishing, Earlene Long

Fingerplay: The Bear Hunt. (Source: *Children's Counting-Out Rhymes, Fingerplays, Jump-Rope and Bounce-Ball Chants and Other Rhythms,* Gloria T. Delamar)

Craft: Basketball Toss. Basketball is a game that even the youngest children can play. Construct a backboard out of oaktag or posterboard. To this attach paper cups with number scores above each. Using ping-pong balls or just crumbled paper allow the children to score by tossing them in the cups (baskets).

Activity: Magnet Fishing. This takes a bit of preparation beforehand. It will require a small tub or swimming pool, paper fish cut with metal tabs on them, and sticks with string and magnets at the end.
The game can be played in a number of ways:

- Place number scores on certain fish to allow the children to try to get the highest score by catching fish with the high numbers.
- Have certain children try to catch designated colored fish. The first to collect all his color wins.

(Source: *500 Games,* Peter L. Cave)

Song: "A-Hunting We Will Go" (Source: *The Silly Songbook,* Esther L. Nelson)

92 Starting School

Filmstrips: *Just Awful*, BFA Educational Media
Little Monster at School, Listening Library
Timothy Goes to School, Weston Woods
When Will I Read?, Random House, Educational
Enrichment Materials

Film: *Louis James Hates School*, Weston Woods

Books: *The New Teacher*, Miriam Cohen
Debbie Goes to Nursery School, Lois Lenski
My Nursery School, Harlow Rockwell
A Trip Through a School, Jeanne Rowe
Betsy's First Day at Nursery School, Gunilla Wolde

Fingerplay: Ready for School. (Source: *Finger Frolics—Revised*, Liz Cromwell, Dixie Hibner, and John R. Faitel)

Craft: Bear Crayon Box. A simple and useful crayon holder box may be constructed using crayons, paint, and a cupcake liner box. These may be used by the children when they begin school. (Source: *Beginning Crafts for Beginning Readers*, Alice Gilbreath)

Activity: Who Stole the Cookie From the Cookie Jar? This is a simple game done with a chant that goes as follows:

All: Who stole the cookie from the cookie jar?
Leader: (Pointing to one child) Did you steal the cookie from the cookie jar?
Child: Who, me?
All: YES, you!
Child: Not me!
All: Not you? Then who? (Pause)

(Repeat this chant substituting items found at school for the cookie and selecting a new child each time.)

Song: "Mary Had a Little Lamb" (Source: *Sing Hey Diddle Diddle*, Beatrice Harrop)

93 Strangers

Filmstrips:	*Careful with Strangers: On the Alert,* Walt Disney Educational Media
	Careful with Strangers: Shortcut to Trouble, Walt Disney Educational Media
	Careful with Strangers: Sizing Up Strangers, Walt Disney Educational Media
	Little Red Riding Hood, SVE
	Winnie the Pooh on the Way to School: Pooh Meets a Stranger, Walt Disney Educational Media
Film:	*Meeting Strangers: Red Light, Green Light,* Phoenix
Books:	*You Can Say "No",* Betty Boegehold
	Strangers, Dorothy Chlad
	Little Red Riding Hood, Paul Galdone
	Never Talk to Strangers, Irma Joyce
	The Dangers of Strangers, Carole Vogel

Fingerplay: The Stranger.
Two little children walking home from school
   (Hold up two fingers walking across other hand)
They meet a tall man lookin' so cool
   (Bring pointer finger of other hand over to meet others)
The stranger said, "Have an ice cream cone"
   (Hold out imaginary cone)
"NO" shouted the children. (Shout out NO)
And they ran on home. (Have two fingers race over palm.)

Craft: Identification Chart. Have the children make a frame for their own special identification chart. Include on the chart the children's fingerprints and, if possible, use a Poloroid camera to include their picture. The children may present this chart to their parents.

Activity: Police Visitation. Contact the local police department and arrange for an officer to speak to the parents, as well as the children. Have the police do official fingerprints for later identification. Many fingerprints done at home are done incorrectly and become useless when needed for identifying a lost child.

Police will offer the children many suggestions on protecting themselves from strangers, and some departments have films for this age group that you may not be able to get elsewhere.

Some departments might even have a costume of McGruff, the crime dog, and will be able to have an officer come dressed as the dog. This costume is only sold to law enforcement agencies.

Song: "Remember Your Name and Address" (Source: *Reader's Digest Children's Songbook*, William L. Simon)

94 Toys

Filmstrips:	*Alexander and the Wind-Up Mouse,* Random House
	Corduroy, Live Oak Media
	Raggedy Ann and Raggedy Andy, SVE
	Stop that Ball, Random House
	The Toy Soldier, EBEC
Films:	*Ira Sleeps Over,* Phoenix
	A Pocket for Corduroy, Phoenix
	William's Doll, Phoenix
Books:	*Poppy the Panda,* Dick Gackenbach
	Arthur's Honey Bear, Lillian Hoban
	Geraldine's Blanket, Holly Keller
	Ernest and Celestine, Gabrielle Vincent
	William's Doll, Charlotte Zolotow

Fingerplay: Tops. (Source: *Rhymes for Learning Times,* Louise Binder Scott)

Craft: Italian 'Piggy in the Pen'. This is a toy that tests your skills. The 'pig' in this toy is a ping-pong ball, and you must try to get it in the round cylinder while it's still attached with a cord. This is a toy that can be taken anywhere (even the car) to amuse children.

Ms. Fiarotta's book will supply you with a step-by-step instructions and a full-page illustration of the toy itself. (Source: *Sticks and Stones and Ice Cream Cones,* Phyllis Fiarotta)

Activity: Jack-in-the-Box. The jack-in-the-box is a familiar toy to most children at this age and can be used in this game. Have all the children crouch low in a row representing the store jack-in-the-boxes. One child enters the store reciting a verse (supplied in the book below) about choosing the best toy. He will touch each child's head telling him to pop-up or pop-down mixing them up. Anyone who goes in the wrong direction is out, and the final child is the winner. (Source: *New Games to Play,* Juel Krisvoy)

Song:	"Blocks" or "I Roll the Ball" (Source: *Music for Ones and Twos,* Tom Glazer)

95 Toys: Balloons

Filmstrips: *The Big Yellow Balloon*, Spoken Arts
Bill's Balloon Ride, Weston Woods
Hot Air Henry, Random House
The Travels of Babar, Random House

Film: *Teddy Bear's Balloon Trip*, Coronet

Books: *Mine's the Best*, Crosby Bonsall
Georgie and the Runaway Balloon, Robert Bright
Hot Air Henry, Random House
I Don't Care, Marjorie Sharmat
The Well Mannered Balloon, Nancy Willard

Fingerplay: The Young Man from the Moon. (Source: *Finger Frolics—Revised*, Liz Cromwell, Dixie Hibner, and John R. Faitel)

Craft: Around-the-World Balloon. Decorate the lower half of a half-pint container and attach it to a helium-filled balloon. This will make a beautiful hot-air balloon that can be used to play balloon races. (Source: *Pint-Size Fun*, Betsy Pflug)

Activity: Balloon Volleyball. No scoring is required for this activity, omitting winners or losers. Lay a stick or string across the floor to divide the room. Children may hit the large balloon as many times as needed to get it across the line. This allows children to focus on one object and make use of their large motor skills. Many variations of this game can be found in: (Source: *Teacher's Handbook of Children's Games*, Marian Jenks Wirth)

Song: "The Balloon" (Source: *Music for Ones and Twos*, Tom Glazer)

96 Trains

Filmstrips: *The Brave Engineer*, Walt Disney Educational Media
Casey Jones, Weston Woods
Freight Train, Random House, Educational
    Enrichment Materials
The Little Engine That Could, SVE
There's a Train Going By My Window, Spoken Arts

Books: *The Little Train*, Graham Greene
Toot! Toot!, Steven Kroll
The Caboose Who Got Loose, Bill Peet
The Freight Train Book, Jack Pierce
The Story of the Little Red Engine, Diana Ross

Fingerplay: Choo-Choo Train. (Source: *Finger Frolics—Revised*, Liz Cromwell, Dixie Hibner, and John R. Faitel)

Craft: Boxes Can be Trains. Simple milk cartons, cereal boxes, or cookie boxes can be cut open, covered with paper, colored and strung together with string to create a small train. The number of cars depends on the size of the group and materials available. Instructions for a caboose, engine, flat car, passenger and coal cars are available in the source below.

If you want to work as a group on one train, why not try getting larger boxes from the supermarkets and making cars for the train that the children can actually sit in. The same instructions can be used for the larger train. (Source: *Just a Box?*, Goldie Taub Chernoff)

Activity: Choo-Choo Train. As the children recite a given verse, they chug along with another child attaching himself to the train each time. When the train is complete, they go under the bridge (a stick going up and down). Those who are touched by the stick are out of the game and must return to the station. (Source: *New Games to Play*, Juel Krisvoy)

Song: "Down By the Station" (Source: *Singing Time: A Book of Songs for Little Children*, Satis N. Coleman and Alice G. Thom)

97 Weather: Rain

Filmstrips: *The Cat in the Hat,* Random House
Cloudy with a Chance of Meatballs, Live Oak Media
Dandelion, Live Oak Media
A Letter to Amy, Weston Woods
My Red Umbrella, Weston Woods

Books: *The Rain Puddle,* Adelaide Holl
Will It Rain?, Holly Keller
Rain Makes Applesauce, Julian Scheer
Rain Drop Splash, Alvin Tresselt
The Storm Book, Charlotte Zolotow

Fingerplay: Eensy Weensy Spider. (Source: *Rhymes for Fingers and Flanner Boards,* Louise Binder Scott and J.J. Thompson)

Craft: Rainbow Shade Pull. A small cardboard shade pull can be made using such materials as white cardboard, yarn, glue, and colored paper. By cutting the shape of the rainbow from the cardboard it can be used as a base.

The yarn and construction paper can be used to add color and yarn attached to the top. This item can be hung in the home window as a proud result of the child's labor. (Source: *Pack-O-Fun Magazine,* Summer, 1984)

Activity: We Dress for the Weather. Using a collection purchased (source below) or a homemade felt collection, have the children dress felt figures of boys and girls with clothes that they should wear when it's raining. (Source: *We Dress for the Weather*—kit, published by the Instructo Corporation)

Song: "It Ain't Gonna Rain No More" (Source: *The Reader's Digest Children's Songbook,* William L. Simon)

98 Weather: Snow

Filmstrips: *The Big Snow*, Weston Woods
Snow, Random House
The Snowy Day, Weston Woods
The Summer Snowman, Random House
White Snow, Bright Snow, Weston Woods

Film: *The Snowman*, Weston Woods

Books: *The Magic Sled*, Nathaniel Benchley
Katy and the Big Snow, Virginia Burton
When Will It Snow?, Syd Hoff
Mike's House, Julia Sauer
White Snow, Bright Snow, Alvin Tresselt

Fingerplay: Snowflakes. (Source: *Hand Rhymes*, Marc Brown)

Craft: Bottled Snow. You will need small baby food jars for this, among other items. Children have seen in stores the small toys you shake up, and it gives you a beautiful snow scene. Well, how about making your own? It's not that difficult, and the child has that feeling of accomplishment.

Silver glitter can make a beautiful snow scene. Let the children draw their own scenery or cut it from a magazine, and attach it to the exterior of the jar.

Clay on the inside of the jar can let you stick small plastic figures inside. (Source: *Purple Cow to the Rescue*, Ann Cole, Carolyn Haas, and Betty Weinberger)

or

Snow Cones. Try a little refreshment at your storyhour. If you're able to obtain an ice crusher, have the children make their own snow cones. Use canned juices for flavor.

Song: "Frosty, the Snowman" (Source: *The Reader's Digest Children's Songbook*, William L. Simon)

99 Witches

Filmstrips:	*Hansel and Gretel*, EBEC
	Strega Nonna, Weston Woods
	Wilma the Witch, SVE
	Winnie the Witch: The Magic Words, SVE
	A Woggle of Witches, Random House, Miller-Brody
Film:	*Teeny-Tiny and the Witch Woman*, Weston Woods
Books:	*Space Witch*, Don Freeman
	Snow White and the Seven Dwarfs, Jacob Grimm
	The Candy Witch, Steven Kroll
	The Littlest Witch, Jeanne Massey
	Witch Bazooza, Dennis Nolan

Fingerplay: Disappearing Witches. (Source: *Rhymes for Learning Times*, Louise Binder Scott)

Craft: Witch's Hat. A witch cannot be a witch without her easily recognized black hat. Black oaktag is one of the better materials for this project. When these are done, the children can use them in the game listed below. (Source: *Pin It, Tack It, Hang It*, Phyllis and Noel Fiarotta)

Activity: The Witch's Magic Thimble. Let the witch, with her newly-made hat, sit at the table pretending to be asleep with her thimble on the table. The other children sit in a safe area designated as the forest. One by one they attempt to steal the thimble. If the child succeeds he's the new witch; if not he must sit under the table. The goal is to be the witch who captures the most children. (Source: *New Games to Play*, Juel Krisvoy)

Song:	"There Was An Old Witch" (Source: *This is Music*, William R. Sur, Mary R. Tolbert, William R. Fisher, and Adeline McCall)

100 Zoos

Filmstrips: *Curious George Takes a Job*, Random House, Educational
Enrichment Materials
Happy Lion's Treasure, EBEC
If I Ran the Zoo, Random House
Put Me in the Zoo, Random House
Something New at the Zoo, Teaching Resources Films

Films: *Leopold the See-Through Crumbpicker*, Weston Woods
The Mole in the Zoo, Phoenix

Books: *Leopold the See-Through Crumbpicker*, James Flora
Animals at the Zoo, Rose Greydanus
Sammy the Seal, Syd Hoff
The Day the Teacher Went Bananas, James Howe
The Biggest Shadow in the Zoo, Jack Kent
I Was Kissed by a Seal at the Zoo, Helen Palmer

Fingerplay: The Zoo. (Source: *Finger Frolics—Revised*, Liz Cromwell, Dixie Hibner, and John R. Faitel)

Craft: A Zoo. Help the children make their own little zoo with the use of boxes. Directions for a cage, lion, alligator, or an elephant can be found in the source below. These can be made with the use of small boxes from cookies, toothpaste, cakes, that can be gathered quickly and at no expense. A great craft for those groups with small budgets. (Source: *Just a Box?*, Goldie Taub Chernoff)

Activity: We Can Do Anything. This action or a listening game can be adapted by the instructor to suit whatever lesson he's teaching at the time. The children dance in a circle imitating the various types of zoo animals the teacher acts out.

If you need a quiet time, turn it into a listening game. Have the children try to identify and then repeat the animal sound that the leader calls out.

Sheet music for the song is included and can be used for the guitar or piano. (Source: *Game-Songs with Prof Dogg's Troupe*, Harriet Powell)

Song: "The Zoo" (Source: *Music for Ones and Twos*, Tom Glazer)

Appendix A

Bantam Books, Inc.
666 Fifth Avenue
New York, NY 10103
  (212) 765-6500
  (800) 323-9872

Beginner Books
Division of Random House, Inc.
201 East 50th Street
New York, NY 10022
  (212) 751-2600
  (800) 638-6460

Bonim Books
A Division of Hebrew Publishing
Co.
Box 25308
1901 North Walnut Street
Oklahoma City, OK 73125

Bowmar-Noble Publishing Co.
Division of Economy Co.
Box 25308
1901 North Walnut Street
Oklahoma City, OK 73125

Bradbury Press
Affiliate of MacMillan, Inc.
866 Third Avenue
New York, NY 10022
  (212) 702-3598
  (800) 257-5755

Carolrhoda Books, Inc.
241 First Avenue, North
Minneapolis, MN 55401
  (612) 332-3344
  (800) 328-4929

Children's Press
1224 West Van Buren Street
Chicago, IL 60607
  (312) 666-4200
  (800) 621-1115

B. Collins
2080 West 117th Street
Cleveland, OH 44111

Communication Skill Builders
3830 East Bellevue
Box 42050
Tucson, AZ 85733
  (602) 323-7500

Coward
  See Putnam Publishing Group

Crowell
  See Harper & Row

Crown Publications, Inc.
225 Park Avenue South
New York, NY 10003
  (212) 254-1600
  (800) 526-4264

Dandelion House
Division of Child's World, Inc.
Box 989
Elgin, IL 60121
  (312) 741-7591

Delacorte Press
1 Dag Hammarskjold Plaza
New York, NY 10017
  (212) 605-3000
  (800) 221-4676

T.S. Denison & Co., Inc.
9601 Newton Avenue South
Minneapolis, MN 55431
  (612) 888-1460
  (800) 328-3831

Deutsch, Andre
  See E.P. Dutton

Dial Books for Young Readers
Division of E.P. Dutton
2 Park Avenue
New York, NY 10016
  (212) 725-1818
  (800) 526-0275

Dillon Press, Inc.
242 Portland Avenue South
Minneapolis, MN 55415
  (612) 333-2691
  (800) 328-8322

Dodd, Mead & Co.
71 Fifth Avenue
New York, NY 10036
  (212) 627-8444
  (800) 237-3255

Doubleday and Co., Inc.
Division of Bertelsman, Inc.
245 Park Avenue
New York, NY 10017
  (212) 984-7561
  (800) 645-6156

E.P. Dutton
Division of NAL/Penguin Inc.
2 Park Avenue
New York, NY 10016
  (212) 725-1818
  (800) 526-0275

Farrar, Straus & Giroux, Inc.
19 Union Square West
New York, NY 10036
  (212) 741-6900
  (800) 242-7737

Follet Corp.
1010 West Washington Blvd.
Chicago, IL 60607

Four Winds Publishing
50 West 44th Street
New York, NY 10036
  (916) 966-7526

G & H Publishing Co.
42 Cornell Drive
Plainview, NY 11803

Garrard Publishing Co.
29 Goldsborough Street
Easton, MD 21601
  (217) 352-7685

Golden Press
  See Western Publishing

Greenwillow Books
Division of William Morrow &
Co., Inc.
105 Madison Avenue
New York, NY 10016
  (212) 889-3050
  (800) 631-1199

Grosset & Dunlap
  See Putnam Publishing Group

Gryphon House, Inc.
Box 275
Mount Rainier, MD 20712
  (301) 779-6200
  (800) 638-0928

Harcourt Brace Jovanovich, Inc.
1250 Sixth Avenue
San Diego, CA 92101
  (619) 699-6335
  (800) 543-1918

Harper & Row Junior Books
Division of Harper & Row
  Publishers, Inc.
10 East 53rd Street
New York, NY 10022
  (212) 207-7000
  (800) 242-7737

Hastings House Publishers
c/o Kampmann & Co., Inc.
10 East 40th Street
New York, NY 10016
  (212) 685-2928
  (800) 526-7626

Henry Holt & Co.
521 Fifth Avenue
New York, NY 10175
  (212) 599-7600

Holiday House, Inc.
18 East 53rd Street
New York, NY 10022
  (212) 688-0085

Houghton Mifflin Co.
1 Beacon Street
Boston, MA 02108
  (617) 725-5000
  (800) 343-1316

Human Sciences Press, Inc.
72 Fifth Avenue
New York, NY 10011
  (212) 243-6000

Incentive Publications, Inc.
3835 Cleghorn Avenue
Nashville, TN 37215
  (615) 385-2934
  (800) 421-2830

Instructor Books
757 Third Avenue
New York, NY 10017

Jewish Publications Society
1930 Chestnut Street
Philadelphia, PA 19103
  (215) 564-5925

Kar-Ben Copies, Inc.
6800 Tildenwood Lane
Rockville, MD 20852
  (301) 984-8733
  (800) 452-7236

Alfred A. Knopf, Inc.
Subsidiary of Random House, Inc.
201 East 50th Street
New York, NY 10022
  (212) 751-2600
  (800) 638-6460

Carl J. Leibel, Inc.
1236 South Hatcher Avenue
Puente, CA

Lerner Publications Co.
241 First Avenue North
Minneapolis, MN 55401
  (612) 332-3344
  (800) 328-4929

J.B. Lippincott Co.
Subsidiary of Harper & Row
  Publishers, Inc.
East Washington Square
Philadelphia, PA 19105
  (215) 238-4200
  (800) 242-7737

Little, Brown & Co.
Division of Time, Inc.
34 Beacon Street
Boston, MA 02108
  (617) 227-0730
  (800) 343-9204

Lothrop, Lee & Shepard Books
Division of William Morrow &
    Co. Inc.
105 Madison Avenue
New York, NY   10016
    (212) 889-3050
    (800) 631-1199

MacMillan Publishing Co., Inc.
866 Third Avenue
New York, NY   10022
    (212) 702-2000
    (800) 257-5755

McFarland & Co., Inc.
Box 611
Jefferson, NC 28640

McGraw-Hill Book Co.
Division of McGraw-Hill, Inc.
1221 Avenue of the Americas
New York, NY   10020
    (212) 512-2000

David McKay, Inc.
Subsidiary of Random House, Inc.
201 East 50th Street
New York, NY   10022
    (212) 751-2600
    (800) 638-6460

Melmont
    See Leibel, Carl, Inc.

Julian Messner
Division of Simon & Schuster, Inc.
1230 Avenue of the Americas
New York, NY   10020
    (212) 698-7000
    (800) 223-1360

M. Evans & Co. Inc.
216 East 49th Street
New York, NY   10017
    (212) 688-2810
    (800) 247-3912

Modern Curriculum Press, Inc.
Division of Simon & Schuster, Inc.
13900 Prospect Road
Cleveland, OH 44136
    (216) 238-2222
    (800) 321-3106

William Morrow & Co., Inc.
Subsidiary of Hearst Corp.
105 Madison Avenue
New York, NY   10016
    (212) 889-3050
    (800) 631-1199

Neugebauer Press USA, Inc.
    See A & C Black

W.W. Norton & Co., Inc.
500 Fifth Avenue
New York, NY   10110
    (212) 354-5500
    (800) 223-2588

Pack-O-Fun, Inc.
14 Main Street
Park Ridge, IL 60068

Pantheon Books
Division of Random House, Inc.
201 East 50th Street
New York, NY   10022
    (212) 751-2600
    (800) 638-6460

Parents Magazine Press
Division of Gruner & Jahr, USA,
  Publishing
685 Third Avenue
New York, NY   10017
  (212) 878-8700

Parker Publishing Co., Inc.
Dept. GC-501
West Nyack, NY 10994

Penguin Books, Inc.
40 West 23rd Street
New York, NY   10010
  (212) 337-5200
  (800) 631-3577

Picture Book Studios USA
60 North Main Street
Natick, MA 01760
  (617) 655-9696
  (800) 462-1252

Prentice Hall Press
Division of Simon & Schuster, a
  Gulf & Western Co.
1 Gulf & Western Plaza
New York, NY   10023
  (212) 373-8500
  (800) 223-2348

Price Stern Sloan Inc.
360 North LaCienega Blvd.
Los Angeles, CA 90048
  (213) 657-6100
  (800) 421-0892

Putnam Publishing Group
200 Madison Avenue
New York, NY   10016
  (212) 576-8900
  (800) 631-8571

Random House, Inc.
201 East 50th Street
New York, NY   10022
  (212) 751-2600
  (800) 638-6460

Reader's Digest Assoc., Inc.
260 Madison Avenue
New York, NY   10016
  (212) 850-7007
  (800) 638-6460

Scholastic Inc.
730 Broadway
New York, NY   10003
  (212) 505-3000
  (800) 257-5755

Charles Scribner's & Sons
866 Third Avenue
New York, NY   10022
  (212) 702-2000
  (800) 257-5755

Silver Burdett & Ginn, Inc.
Division of Simon & Schuster
191 Spring Street
Lexington, MA 02173
  (617) 863-9400
  (800) 631-8081

Simon & Schuster
Children's Book Division
Rockefeller Center
New York, NY   10020

Stackpole Book Co., Inc.
Division of Commonwealth
  Communications, Inc.
Box 1831
Cameron & Kelker Streets
Harrisburg, PA 17105
  (717) 234-5041
  (800) 732-3669

Sterling Publishing Co., Inc.
2 Park Avenue
New York, NY   10016
    (212) 532-7160
    (800) 367-9692

Gareth Stevens Inc.
7317 West Green Tree Road
Milwaukee, WI 53223
    (414) 466-7550
    (800) 341-3567

Teacher Created Materials Inc.
Box 301
Sunset Beach, CA 90742

Transatlantic Arts, Inc.
Box 6086
Albuquerque, NM 87197
    (505) 898-2289

Troll Associates
Subsidiary of Educational Reading
    Services
100 Corporate Drive
Mahwah, NJ 07430
    (201) 549-4000
    (800) 526-5289

Vanguard Press, Inc.
424 Madison Avenue
New York, NY   10017
    (212) 753-3906

Viking Penguin, Inc.
40 West 23rd Street
New York, NY   10010
    (212) 337-5200
    (800) 631-3577

Henry Z. Walck
Division of David McKay Co., Inc.
201 East 50th Street
New York, NY   10022-7703
    (212) 340-9800
    (800) 327-4801

Walker & Co.
Division of Walker Publishing Co.
Inc.
720 Fifth Avenue
New York, NY   10019
    (212) 265-3632

Franklin Watts Inc.
Subsidiary of Grolier, Inc.
387 Park Avenue
New York, NY   10016
    (212) 686-7070
    (800) 672-6672

Western Publishing Co., Inc.
Subsidiary of Western Publishing
    Group, Inc.
850 Third Avenue
New York, NY   10022
    (212) 753-8500

H.W. Wilson
950 University Avenue
Bronx, NY 10452
    (212) 588-8400
    (800) 367-6770

Windmill Books, Inc.
Division of Intext
c/o Simon & Schuster
200 Old Tappan Road
Old Tappan, NJ 07575

Workman Publishing Co., Inc.
1 West 39th Street
New York, NY   10018
    (212) 398-9160
    (800) 722-7202

Zaner-Bloser, Inc.
612 North Park Street
Columbus, OH

Appendix B

Live Oak Media
Box 34
Ancramdale, NY 12503

MacMillan Films
34 MacQuesten Parkway South
Mount Vernon, NY 10550
   (914) 664-5051
   (800) 257-8247

McGraw-Hill, Inc.
1221 Avenue of the Americas
New York, NY 10020

Mulberry Park, Inc.
Box 4096
Dept. B 103
Englewood, CO 80155

Oxford University Press, Inc.
200 Madison Avenue
New York, NY 10016
   (212) 796-8000

Phoenix Films, Inc.
468 Park Avenue South
New York, NY   10016
   (212) 684-5910
   (800) 221-1274

Pied Piper Media
1645 Monrovia Avenue
Costa Mesa, CA 92627
   (800) 247-8308

Random House, Miller-Brody
   Productions
Department 9278
400 Hahn Road
Westminster, MD 21157
   (800) 638-6460

Rembrandt Films
59 East 54th Street
New York, NY 10022

Society for Visual Education, Inc.
Department BL
1345 Diversey Parkway
Chicago, IL 60614
   (800) 621-1900

Spoken Arts, Inc.
310 North Avenue
New Rochelle, NY   10801
   (914) 636-5482

Troll Associates
School and Library Division
100 Corporate Drive
Mahwah, NJ 07430

Walt Disney Educational Media
   See Coronet Films

Weston Woods Productions
Weston Woods, CT 06880

Abbreviations of Filmstrip, Film and Video Distributors

AV	Ambrose Video Publishing, Inc.	LOM	Live Oak Media
BC	Brodart & Co.	MF	MacMillan Films
BFA	BFA Educational Media	MH	McGraw-Hill
BT	Baker & Taylor Video	MP	Mulberry Park, Inc.
CL	Clearvue Inc.	OUP	Oxford University Press
CF	Coronet Films	PF	Phoenix Films
EEM	Educational Enrichment Materials	PPM	Pied Piper Media
EBEC	Encyclopedia Britannica Educational Corporation	RH/MB	Random House, Miller-Brody
EGM	Eye Gate Media	RF	Rembrandt Films
IIL	Imperial International Learning Corporation	SVE	Society for Visual Education, Inc.
LCA	Learning Corporation of America	SA	Spoken Arts, Inc.
LT	Learning Tree Publishing	TA	Troll Associates
LL	Listening Library	WD	Walt Disney Educational Media
		WW	Weston Woods

NOTE: *Numbers refer to sequence numbers of activity, not to page numbers.*

TITLE	C or B & W	DATE	LENGTH	FRAMES	PRICE	PUBLISHER	NUMBER
Adventures of a Kitten	C	1968	5 min.	43	12.00	IIL	6
Alexander & the Wind-Up Mouse	C	1978	7 min.	36	27.50	RH/MB	10,40,92
Alligators All Around	C	1976	4 min.	30	24.00	WW	2,80
Amelia Bedelia	C	1974	10 min.	50	26.00	RH/MB	64
Anatole	C	1978	10 min.	46	39.00	EBEC	10
Andrew & the Strawberry Monster	C	1975	6 min.	62	39.00	EBEC	16,46,72
Andy and the Lion	B&W	---	6 min.	38	24.00	WW	9,28,68
Angus & the Ducks	C	---	6 min.	35	24.00	WW	20
Are You My Mother?	C	1974	5 min.	68	25.00	FH/MB	43
Arthur's Christmas Cookies	C	1980	10 min.	51	39.00	EBEC	54
Arthur's Halloween	C	1982	8 min.	79	25.00	RH/MB	58
Arthur's Pen Pal	C	1978	10 min.	50	39.00	EBEC	11
Arthur's Prize Reader	C	1980	11 min.	51	39.00	EBEC	1
Arthur's Thanksgiving	C	1983	9 min.	73	25.00	RH/MB	61
Ask Mr. Bear	C	1973	5 min.	40	13.00	MF	23
Babar Loses His Crown	C	1974	8 min.	107	25.00	RH/MB	16,83
The Bear Detectives	C	1977	7 min.	95	25.00	RH/MB	5,79
Bear Hunt	C	1981	4 min.	25	30.00	WW	13
The Bears Bicycle	C	1977	4 min.	37	24.95	LOM	18
The Bears Find Thanksgiving	C	1982	7 min.	29	38.50	SVE	61
Bears in the Night	C	1974	4 min.	41	25.00	RH/MB	75
Bears on Wheels	C	1975	3 min.	33	25.00	RH/MB	35
The Bears Vacation	C	1974	6 min.	53	25.00	RH/MB	84,85,88
The Bear Who Slept Through Christmas	C	1982	8 min.	27	38.50	SVE	54
Bedtime for Frances	C	1978	13 min.	64	22.00	BFA	15

TITLE	C or B &W	DATE	LENGTH	FRAMES	PRICE	PUBLISHER	NUMBER
The Best Mom in the World	C	1981	7 min.	56	26.00	RH/MB	43
Bicycle Safety: Safety on Wheels with Goofy	C	1977	8 min.	65	33.00	WD	18,84
Big Bear to the Rescue	C	1978	8 min.	50	39.00	EBEC	5
Big Dog...Little Dog	C	1974	4 min.	51	25.00	RH/MB	34
The Biggest Bear	C	----	7 min.	48	24.00	WW	28,77
The Biggest House in the World	C	1978	5 min.	33	25.00	RH/MB	34,63
The Big Honey Hunt	C	1977	8 min.	110	25.00	RH/MB	46
The Big Snow	C	1974	11 min.	53	24.00	WW	89, 98
The Big Yellow Balloon	C	1968	15 min.	63	18.50	SA	96
The Bike Lesson	C	1975	7 min.	70	25.00	RH/MB	18
Bill's Balloon Ride	C	----	9 min.	32	24.00	WW	95
A Birthday for Frances	C	1978	16 min.	75	22.00	BFA	23
The Birthday Trombone	C	1978	7 min.	40	39.00	EBEC	23,73,81
Bootle Beatle	C	1977	12 min.	72	37.00	WD	66
The Box with the Red Wheels	C	1973	5 min.	40	14.00	MF	14
The Boy Who Didn't Like Thanksgiving	C	1975	11 min.	60	32.00	EGM	61
The Boy Who Would Not Say His Name	C	1977	6 min	32	26.00	RH/MB	74
The Brave Engineer	C	1977	12 min.	65	37.00	WD	96
The Bremen-Town Musicians	C	1980	11 min.	74	27.50	RH/MB	73,76
The Bunnies Easter Surprise	C	1975	6 min.	67	15.50	SVE	55
The Butter Battle Book	C	1984	14 min.	119	25.00	RH/MB	39
The Camel with the Wrinkled Knees	C	1978	10 min.	41	18.50	SVE	4
Caps for Sale	C	----	6 min.	34	24.00	WW	31
Careful with Strangers: On the Alert	C	1977	13 min.	68	36.00	WD	93
Careful with Strangers: Sizing up Strangers	C	1977	10 min.	73	36.00	WD	93
Careful with Strangers: Shortcut to Trouble	C	1977	13 min.	79	36.00	WD	93

TITLE	C or B&W	DATE	LENGTH	FRAMES	PRICE	PUBLISHER	NUMBER
Casey Jones	C	----	5 min.	19	24.00	WW	96
The Cat in the Hat	C	1974	10 min.	137	25.00	RH/MB	6,31,97
Cecily G. and the 9 Monkeys	C	1978	12 min.	52	26.00	RH/MB	11
Check it Out	C	1985	7 min.	65	24.95	LL	68
The Circus Baby	C	1950	6 min.	35	24.00	WW	29,70
C is for Clown	C	1978	4 min.	35	25.00	RH/MB	29
Cloudy with a Chance of Meatballs	C	1985	12 min.	49	24.95	LOM	76,97
The Cold Blooded Penguin	C	1974	8 min.	75	37.00	WD	22
Corduroy	C	1970	5 min.	34	24.95	LOM	30,40,94
Crictor	C	1981	6 min.	31	24.00	WW	81
Curious George	C	1971	7 min.	60	26.00	RH/MB	11,26
Curious George Flies a Kite	C	1971	14 min.	120	26.00	RH/MB	67
Curious George Goes to the Hospital	C	1971	10 min.	60	26.00	RH/MB	62
Curious George Learns the Alphabet	C	1977	17 min.	118	72.00	RH/MB	2
Curious George Rides a Bike	C	1974	10 min.	58	24.00	WW	29
Curious George Takes a Job	C	1971	7 min.	60	26.00	RH/MB	100
Dandelion	C	1970	5 min.	46	24.95	LOM	9,97
Danny and the Dinosaur	C	1974	8 min.	60	24.00	WW	37
The Day After Mother's Day	C	1975	11 min.	59	32.00	EGM	43
The Day Jimmy's Boa Ate the Wash	C	1985	5 min.	35	24.00	WW	64,81
Dinnay and Danny	C	1974	7 min.	44	14.00	MF	37
Dinosaur Tales: Baby Horned-Faced & the Egg Stealer	C	1976	16 min.	65	19.00	CF	37
Dr. DeSoto	C	1982	9 min.	47	24.00	WW	25
Dumbo	C	1974	22 min.	150	74.00	WD	8

TITLE	C or B &W	DATE	LENGTH	FRAMES	PRICE	PUBLISHER	NUMBER
The Ear Book	C	1974	4 min.	36	25.00	RH/MB	3
The Easter Basket Mystery	C	1977	10 min.	55	35.00	SVE	55
Easter Bunnyland	C	----	4 min.	33	36.00	WD	55
Earth Day & the Galaxy Gnomes	C	----	9 min.	38	30.00	CL	90
The Elves & the Shoemaker	C	1968	11 min.	45	33.00	EBEC	59
Emil, The Tap Dancing Frog	C	1975	8 min.	49	39.00	EBEC	50,73
The Emperor & the Kite	C	1976	8 min.	49	24.95	LL	67
The Emperor's New Clothes	C	----	9 min.	69	39.00	EBEC	30,64,65,83
The Eye Book	C	1974	5 min.	44	25.00	RH/MB	3
Fat Magic	C	1980	9 min.	51	39.00	EBEC	69
Finding What You Want (Lollipop Dragon)	C	1983	10 min.	46	38.50	SVE	68
Fish Is Fish	C	1974	4 min.	67	25.00	RH/MB	45
A Fish Out of Water	C	1978	12 min.	114	25.00	RH/MB	45
The Five Chinese Brothers	C	----	10 min.	56	24.00	WW	48
A Fly Went By	C	1975	11 min.	101	25.00	RH/MB	66
The Fractured Turtle	C	1972	5 min.	43	12.00	IIL	82
Frederick	C	1973	5 min.	47	27.50	RH/MB	10
Frederick's Alligator	C	1980	5 min.	51	39.00	EBEC	80
Freight Train	C	1980	5 min.	63	27.50	RH/MB	32,96
Frog and Toad Are Friends: A Swim	C	1976	6 min.	36	27.50	RH/MB	88,91
Frog and Toad Are Friends: Spring	C	1976	6 min.	34	27.50	RH/MB	87
Frog and Toad Are Friends: The Story	C	1976	6 min.	38	27.50	RH/MB	50
Frog and Toad Together: Dragons and Giants	C	1976	5 min.	36	30.00	RH/MB	38,52
Frog and Toad Together: The Garden	C	1976	5 min.	33	30.00	RH/MB	78
The Frog Prince	C	1972	5 min.	43	12.00	SA	50
Funny Feet	C	1981	5 min.	38	26.00	RH/MB	3,22,30
Georgie	C	1974	6 min.	40	24.00	WW	51

TITLE	C or B&W	DATE	LENGTH	FRAMES	PRICE	PUBLISHER	NUMBER
The Ghost with the Halloween Hiccups	C	1979	5 min.	39	26.00	RH/MB	51,58
The Gingerbread Boy	C	1970	8 min.	41	14.00	CF	42
Goodnight Owl!	C	1982	4 min.	31	24.00	WW	15,21,75
The Grasshopper & the Ants	C	1977	15 min.	75	34.00	WD	66
Green Eggs & Ham	C	1974	6 min.	77	25.00	RH/MB	46
Groundhog's Day	C	1980	7 min.	35	35.00	SVE	57
Hand, Hand, Fingers, Thumb	C	1978	5 min.	44	25.00	RH/MB	3,11
Hansel and Gretel	C	1968	11 min.	45	33.00	RH/MB	99
Hanukkah	C	----	12 min.	63	39.00	EBEC	53
Hanukkah Hot Cakes	C	1982	7 min.	39	35.00	SVE	53
The Happy Lion's Rabbits	C	1978	8 min.	50	39.00	EBEC	12
Happy Lion's Treasure	C	1978	12 min.	56	39.00	EBEC	9,100
The Happy Owls	C	----	4 min.	21	24.00	WW	21,40
Harold and the Purple Crayon	C	1974	7 min.	64	24.00	WW	13,32,64,65
Harry and the Lady Next Door	C	1977	14 min.	88	25.00	RH/MB	75
Harry By the Sea	C	1977	10 min.	69	25.00	RH/MB	85
Harry the Dirty Dog	C	1977	7 min.	53	25.00	RH/MB	77
Harry the Hider	C	1980	5 min.	33	23.25	IIL	6,29
The Hat	C	1981	9 min.	45	24.00	WW	31
Hector & Christina	C	1978	10 min.	50	39.00	EBEC	22
Hector Penguin	C	1978	12 min.	42	39.00	EBEC	22
Henny Penny	C	1970	7 min.	44	14.00	CF	4,42,44
Henry the Explorer	C	1977	6 min.	34	24.00	WW	89
Hercules	C	1974	11 min.	52	24.00	WW	26
Holidays: Independence Day	C	1977	13 min.	75	25.00	RH/MB	56
Hooper Humperdink..? Not Him!	C	1978	9 min.	79	25.00	RH/MB	2,23,74
Horton Hatches an Egg	C	1976	14 min.	117	48.75	RH/MB	8,19,28,79
Hot Air Henry	C	1985	12 min.	88	26.00	RH/MB	95
The House on East 88th Street	C	----	10 min.	63	24.00	RH/MB	63

TITLE	C or B&W	DATE	LENGTH	FRAMES	PRICE	PUBLISHER	NUMBER
How Mother Possum Got Her Pouch	C	----	9 min.	35	39.00	EBEC	41
How Not to Catch a Mouse	C	1974	10 min.	68	17.00	BFA	10
How the Trollusk Got His Hat	C	1982	6 min.	52	24.95	LL	31
How the Woodpecker Got His Feathers	C	----	9 min.	35	39.00	EBEC	41
Hunches in Bunches	C	1982	7 min.	75	26.00	RH/MB	12
Hush Little Baby	C	1970	3 min.	17	24.00	WW	14
I Can Read with My Eyes Shut	C	1978	8 min.	65	25.00	RH/MB	1
If I Ran the Zoo	C	1977	19 min.	142	49.50	RH/MB	100
The Iguana Who Was Always Right	C	----	12 min.	66	39.00	EBEC	47
I Know an Old Lady Who Swallowed a Fly	C	1983	10 min.	78	24.95	LL	46,73,76
I'll Teach My Dog 100 Words	C	1974	5 min.	66	25.00	RH/MB	79
I'm No Fool in Water	C	1977	7 min.	59	33.00	WD	85
I'm No Fool with a Bicycle	C	1977	7 min.	64	33.00	WD	18
I'm No Fool with Fire	C	1977	8 min.	72	33.00	WD	26,84
I'm No Fool with Poisons	C	1977	9 min.	79	33.00	WD	84
Indians for Thanksgiving	C	1966	11 min.	49	35.00	SVE	61
Ira Sleeps Over	C	1984	14 min.	57	24.95	LOM	15
I Wish I Had Duck Feet	C	1975	8 min.	75	25.00	RH/MB	17
Jack and the Beanstalk	C	1968	11 min.	45	33.00	EBEC	52,78
Johnny's Birthday Wish	C	----	9 min.	38	29.00	CL	17
Johnny, The Fireman	C	1972	7 min.	63	11.50	SVE	26
Josie and the Snow	C	----	3 min.	26	24.00	WW	89
July Fourth and Summer Safety	C	1977	6 min.	55	36.00	WD	56,88
King of the Forest	C	----	12 min.	80	39.00	EBEC	48
The King's Favorite Easter Egg Contest	C	1975	12 min.	59	32.00	EGM	55
The King, the Mice & the Cheese	C	1974	7 min.	61	25.00	RH/MB	83

TITLE	C or B&W	DATE	LENGTH	FRAMES	PRICE	PUBLISHER	NUMBER
A Kiss for Little Bear	C	1973	4 min.	35	24.00	WW	5,60
The Kite Ride	C	1979	8 min.	34	19.00	SVE	67
Lambert, the Sheepish Lion	C	1974	8 min.	81	37.00	WD	9
The Lavender Leprechaun	C	----	7 min.	50	37.00	WD	59
The Legend of Sleepy Hollow	C	----	17 min.	140	74.00	WD	51
Lentil	C	----	9 min.	41	24.00	WW	35,75
Let's Find Out About Fall	C	1977	6 min.	37	25.00	RH/MB	86
Let's Find Out About Spring	C	1977	5 min.	41	25.00	RH/MB	87
A Letter to Amy	C	1970	6 min.	38	24.00	WW	97
Library Manners for Primaries: Shh..Quiet Please	C	1982	7 min.	46	33.00	EGM	68
Little Burnt Face	C	----	12 min.	66	39.00	EBEC	41
The Little Engine That Could	C	1977	11 min.	59	25.00	SVE	96
Little Fox Goes to the End of the World	C	1980	7 min.	34	23.25	IIL	4
The Little House	C	1974	8 min.	64	37.00	WD	39,63
Little Monster at Home	C	1982	6 min.	53	24.95	LL	63
Little Monster at School	C	1982	6 min.	54	24.95	LL	92
Little Monster's Counting Book	C	1982	8 min.	70	24.95	LL	35
Little Rabbit's Loose Tooth	C	1984	10 min.	55	30.00	PPM	12
The Little Red Hen	C	1970	8 min.	41	14.00	CF	19,44
The Little Red Lighthouse the Great Gray Bridge	C	----	9 min.	42	24.00	WW	24
Little Red Riding Hood	C	----	10 min.	40	15.00	SVE	42,93
Little Tim & the Brave Sea Captain	C	----	9 min.	58	24.00	WW	24,85
Little Toot	C	----	10 min.	52	24.00	WW	24
Lollipop Dragon Helps Santa	C	1971	9 min.	55	38.50	SVE	54
Lollipop Dragon's First Halloween	C	1971	8 min.	44	38.50	SVE	58
Lollipop Dragon's Mother's Day Surprise	C	1971	8 min.	36	38.50	SVE	43

TITLE	C or B&W	DATE	LENGTH	FRAMES	PRICE	PUBLISHER	NUMBER
Lollipop Dragon's Valentine Party	C	1971	8 min.	50	38.50	SVE	60
The Lorax	C	1977	21 min.	175	48.75	RH/MB	39,71
Lyle and the Birthday Party	C	1971	15 min.	71	27.00	RH/MB	23,62
Lyle, Lyle Crocodile	C	1971	11 min.	82	27.50	RH/MB	80
Madeline	C	1985	7 min.	80	27.50	RH/MB	62
Madeline's Rescue	C	1953	6 min.	53	24.00	WW	79
The Magical Drawings of Mooney B. Finch	C	----	10 min.	54	24.95	LL	13
Magic Fishbone	C	1977	14 min.	66	24.95	LL	69
The Magic Porridge Pot	C	1981	5 min.	32	24.95	LL	69
Make Way for Ducklings	C	----	11 min.	47	24.00	WW	20,27
Meet Babar and His Family	C	1974	5 min.	75	25.00	RH/MB	8
A Merry Mouse Book of Months	C	1981	5 min.	26	38.50	SVE	36
A Merry Mouse Christmas A-B-C	C	1981	5 min.	26	38.50	SVE	2
Mickey and the Beanstalk	C	1974	13 min.	73	37.00	WD	52,78
Mickey Mouse, The Brave Little Tailor	C	1974	7 min.	62	37.00	WD	10,52
The Monkey King	C	----	6 min.	30	35.00	SVE	48
Monster Seeds	C	1975	6 min.	58	39.00	EBEC	72,78
Morris' Disappearing Bag	C	1978	6 min.	38	24.00	WW	54
Monsters in the Closet	C	1975	6 min.	63	39.00	EBEC	72
Mothers Can Do Anything	C	1980	5 min.	45	24.00	IIL	43
Mother, Mother I Want Another	C	1980	5 min.	37	23.25	IIL	15
Mouskin Finds a Friend	C	----	5 min.	30	26.00	RH/MB	49
Mr. Gumpy's Outing	C	1973	5 min.	27	24.00	WW	24
Mr. Terwilliger's Secret	C	1981	5 min.	37	26.00	RH/MB	37
My Friend from Outer Space	C	1981	7 min.	50	26.00	RH/MB	65,90
My Red Umbrella	C	1972	4 min.	28	24.00	WW	97

TITLE	C or B&W	DATE	LENGTH	FRAMES	PRICE	PUBLISHER	NUMBER
The Neatos & the Litterbugs	C	1974	5 min.	40	25.00	RH/MB	39
Noisy Nora	C	1975	10 min.	28	24.00	WW	75
No One Noticed Ralph	C	1980	9 min.	65	23.25	IIL	19
Norman the Doorman	C	1959	11 min.	55	24.00	WW	13
No Roses for Harry	C	1977	9 min.	64	25.00	RH/MB	7, 30
Oh, Were They Ever Happy	C	1979	4 min.	32	24.95	LL	32,63
Old Blue	C	1975	7 min.	44	39.00	EBEC	76
Old Hat, New Hat	C	1978	4 min.	45	25.00	RH/MB	30,31,33,34
Old Mother Hubbard and Her Dog	C	1977	5 min.	35	24.00	WW	76
One Fish, Two Fish, Red Fish, Blue Fish	C	1974	12 min.	130	25.00	RH/MB	45
One Monday Morning	C	1973	7 min.	31	24.00	WW	36
One Was Johnny	C	1976	3 min.	26	24.00	WW	35
One Zillion Valentines	C	1984	6 min.	133	25.00	RH/MB	60
The Owl and the Grasshopper	C	---	10 min.	65	25.00	RH/MB	21
Paddington Helps Out: Paddington Dines Out	C	1983	5 min.	39	30.00	LT	5
People Do Different Kinds of Work, Charlie Brown	C	1979	7 min.	67	25.00	RH/MB	27
Peter's Chair	C	1967	4 min.	27	24.00	WW	14
Pete's Dragon	C	1979	29 min.	248	74.00	WD	38
Pet Stories: The Parakeet Who Panicked	C	1976	7 min.	60	39.00	EBEC	77
Petunia	C	---	12 min.	50	24.00	WW	1
Petunia, Beware	C	1974	7 min.	81	25.00	RH/MB	19,44
A Picture For Harold's Room	C	1974	6 min.	61	24.00	WW	13
Play Ball, Amelia Bedelia	C	---	10 min.	65	26.00	RH/MB	91
Pluto's Fledgling	C	1977	15 min.	77	34.00	WD	82
Pluto's Surprise Package	C	---	8 min.	60	37.00	WD	7
The Pokey Little Puppy	C	1974	7 min.	72	25.00	RH/MB	7
The Poor Woodcutter & the Dove	C	1978	5 min.	50	39.00	EBEC	17
Pretzel	C	1978	5 min.	35	26.00	RH/MB	7

TITLE	C or B&W	DATE	LENGTH	FRAMES	PRICE	PUBLISHER	NUMBER
Private Zoo	C	1976	6 min.	38	24.95	LOM	57
Put Me in the Zoo	C	1974	5 min.	57	25.00	RH/MB	70,100
Rackety Rabbit and the Runaway Easter Eggs	C	1966	9 min.	29	35.00	SVE	55
Raggedy Ann & Fido	C	1979	8 min.	36	19.00	SVE	7
Raggedy Ann & Raggedy Andy	C	1979	10 min.	41	38.50	SVE	94
Raggedy Ann Learns a Lesson	C	1978	9 min.	42	35.50	SVE	60
The Reluctant	C	1975	12 min.	103	36.00	WD	38
Roses are Red, Are Violets Blue?	C	1974	7 min.	102	25.00	RH/MB	32
Rumpelstilskin	C	1968	11 min.	45	33.00	EBEC	42,69,74
The Saggy Baggy Elephant	C	1977	8 min.	46	18.00	RH/MB	8
St. Patrick's Day	C	1980	6 min.	37	35.00	SVE	59
Sam and the Firefly	C	1974	10 min.	91	25.00	RH/MB	21,66
Sam Shape and the Clumsy Car	C	----	7 min.	35	30.00	CL	33
The Shape of Me & Other Stuff	C	1978	7 min.	54	25.00	RH/MB	33
Shapesville "Shapes Up"	C	----	7 min.	35	30.00	CL	33
Snakes	C	----	6 min.	38	29.00	CL	81
Snow	C	1978	9 min.	79	25.00	RH/MB	89,98
Snow White and the 7 Dwarfs	C	1974	15 min.	120	72.00	WD	59
The Snowy Day	C	1974	6 min.	27	24.00	WW	98
Someday	C	1976	4 min.	33	26.00	RH/MB	17
Springtime for Jeanne-Marie	C	1974	7 min.	44	25.00	RH/MB	20,87
The Story of Hanukkah and Christmas	C	1964	12 min.	43	35.00	SVE	53
The Story of Little Thumb	C	1965	13 min.	55	36.00	EBEC	34
The Story of Ping	C	---- -	10 min.	45	24.00	WW	20,48
The Story of Puss in Boots	C	1965	13 min.	53	36.00	EBEC	6
The Story of the Little Mermaid	C	1965	13 min.	52	36.00	EBEC	71
The Summer Snowman	C	1977	8 min.	44	25.00	RH/MB	56,88,98
Swimmy	C	1973	3 min.	30	27.50	RH/MB	45

TITLE	C or B&W	DATE	LENGTH	FRAMES	PRICE	PUBLISHER	NUMBER
Tawny Scrawny Lion	C	1974	7 min.	62	25.00	RH/MB	9
Ten Apples Up On Top	C	1974	5 min.	72	25.00	RH/MB	35
Thanksgiving in Tumtum	C	1971	9 min.	63	38.50	SVE	61
Thank You Amelia Bedelia	C	----	10 min.	43	26.00	RH/MB	70
Theodore	C	1974	10 min.	36	17.00	BFA	28
There's a Hippopotamus Under My Bed	C	1979	4 min.	38	26.00	RH/MB	4
There's a Nightmare in My Closet	C	1982	4 min.	35	24.95	LL	15,40,72
There's a Train Going By My Window	C	1982	5 min.	39	22.00	SA	96
The Three Funny Friends	C	1976	4 min.	34	26.00	RH/MB	49
Three Little Kittens	C	1974	4 min.	61	25.00	RH/MB	16
The Three Little Pigs	C	1981	9 min.	41	24.00	WW	4
Thumbelina	C	----	10 min.	34	24.95	LOM	34
Tikki Tikki Tembo	C	1970	8 min.	32	24.00	WW	48,74
Timothy Goes to School	C	1981	6 min.	35	24.00	WW	49,92
The Tortoise and the Hare	C	1974	8 min.	62	37.00	WD	12,82,91
The Toy Soldier	C	1968	9 min.	43	39.00	EBEC	95
Trick or Treat	C	----	7 min.	85	37.00	WD	58
The Turnip	C	1973	5 min.	40	15.00	MF	44,78
Two Hundred Rabbits	C	1972	12 min.	34	24.95	LOM	12
The Ugly Duckling	C	1974	8 min.	62	37.00	WD	19,20
Under the Rainbow	C	1970	12 min.	58	22.00	RH/MB	32
A Visit to the Dentist	C	1981	8 min.	58	36.00	WD	25
A Visit to the Hospital	C	----	8 min.	45	38.50	SVE	62
What Do You Do Dear?	C	1974	5 min.	27	24.00	WW	70
What Do You Say Dear?	C	1974	5 min.	27	24.00	WW	70
When Will I Read?	C	1980	5 min.	31	26.00	RH/MB	1,92
Where Can An Elephant Hide?	C	1982	8 min.	51	22.00	SA	8
Where The Wild Things Are	C	1975	5 min.	38	24.00	WW	65,72
White Snow, Bright Snow	C	1947	7 min.	36	24.00	WW	98
Wilma the Witch	C	1968	8 min.	39	12.00	IIL	99
Winnie the Pooh & the Blustery Day	C	1974	22 min.	150	74.00	WD	86

TITLE	C or B&W	DATE	LENGTH	FRAMES	PRICE	PUBLISHER	NUMBER
Winnie the Pooh & Tigger Too!	C	1977	21 min.	200	74.00	WD	5
Winnie the Pooh Discovers the Seasons: Pooh & Owl Have a Fall Adventure	C	1981	8 min.	50	37.00	WD	86
Winnie the Pooh Discovers the Seasons: Pooh Catches Spring Fever	C	1981	6 min.	50	37.00	WD	87
Winnie the Pooh on the Way to School: Pooh Meets a Stranger	C	1977	12 min.	70	34.00	WD	93
Winnie the Pooh on the Way to School: Rabbit Has a Bicycle Ride	C	1977	14 min.	64	34.00	WD	18
Wimmie the Pooh on the Way to School: Tigger Becomes a Pedestrian	C	1977	10 min.	70	34.00	WD	84
Winnie the Witch & the Frightened Ghost	C	1974	8 min.	51	38.50	SVE	51
Winnie the Witch: The Magic Words	C	1975	13 min.	55	38.50	SVE	99
A Woggle of Witches	C	1974	6 min.	36	25.00	RH/MB	99
The Worst Person in the World	C	1980	10 min.	46	23.25	IIL	49
Would You Rather Be a Bullfrog?	C	1978	8 min.	74	25.00	RH/MB	50
Yertle the Turtle	C	1977	12 min.	76	42.50	RH/MB	82
You Can't Put Braces on Spaces	C	1981	10 min.	70	26.00	RH/MB	25
You May Like Many Jobs, Charlie Brown	C	1979	6 min.	69	25.00	RH/MB	27

TITLE	C or B & W	DATE	LENGTH	RENTAL	PRICE	PUBLISHER	NUMBER
The Amazing Bone	C	1985	11 min.	25.00	245.00	WW	69
Anatole and the Piano	C	1968	12 min.	20.00	195.00	MH	10
Andy and the Lion	C	1955	10 min.	20.00	195.00	WW	68
Angus Lost	C	1982	11 min.	25.00	260.00	PF	7
The Ant and the Dove	C	----	8 min.	35.00	205.00	CF	66
The Bear and the Fly	C	1984	5 min.	15.00	125.00	WW	5
Blueberries for Sal	C	1967	9 min.	20.00	175.00	WW	5
A Boy, A Dog and a Frog	C	1981	9 min.	20.00	210.00	PF	50,7
A Boy and a Boa	C	1975	13 min.	25.00	275.00	PF	81
The Camel Who Took a Walk	C	1957	6 min.	20.00	140.00	WW	4
Caps for Sale	C	1960	5 min.	15.00	115.00	WW	64,11
Charlie Needs a Cloak	C	1976	8 min.	20.00	195.00	WW	30
Circus Baby	C	1956	5 min.	15.00	115.00	WW	8
Curious George Rides a Bike	C	1958	10 min.	20.00	195.00	WW	18
Dorothy and the Ostrich	C	1982	9 min.	19.00	200.00	PF	19
Draghetto	C	1979	12 min.	20.00	235.00	PF	26,38
Dragon Stew	C	1972	13 min.	43.00	295.00	PF	38,46
The Elephant's Child	C	----	12 min.	40.00	260.00	CF	8
The First Easter Rabbit	C	----	25 min.	60.00	525.00	CF	55
The Fisherman and His Wife	C	1977	20 min.	30.00	375.00	WW	45
The Five Chinese Brothers	C	1958	10 min.	20.00	195.00	WW	48
Frog Goes to Dinner	C	1985	12 min.	35.00	300.00	PF	46
The Frog Princess	C	----	6 min.	35.00	160.00	CF	50
Frog Went A-Courtin'	C	1961	12 min.	25.00	235.00	WW	50,73
Georgie	C	1956	6 min.	20.00	140.00	WW	58
The Giant Devil-Dingo	C	1985	10 min.	20.00	195.00	WW	52
Grandfather's Mittens	C	1975	10 min.	17.00	210.00	PF	63

TITLE	C or B&W	DATE	LENGTH	RENTAL	PRICE	PUBLISHER	NUMBER
Happy Birthday Moon	C	1985	7 min.	20.00	175.00	WW	23
Harold's Fairy Tale	C	1974	8 min.	20.00	195.00	WW	42
Helpful Little Fireman	C	----	11 min.	40.00	255.00	CF	26
How the Leopard Got His Spots	C	----	11 min.	40.00	260.00	CF	47
How the Whale Got His Throat	C	----	11 min.	40.00	260.00	CF	45
In the Night Kitchen	C	----	6 min.	20.00	175.00	WW	65
Ira Sleeps Over	C	1977	17 min.	30.00	295.00	PF	49,94
Jonah and the Great Fish	C	1987	6 min.	20.00	140.00	WW	45
Ladybug, Ladybug, Winter is Coming!	C	----	10 min.	40.00	250.00	CF	87
Lentil	C	1957	9 min.	20.00	175.00	WW	73
Leo on Vacation	C	1975	11 min.	20.00	230.00	PF	9
Leopold the See-Through Crumbpicker	C	1971	9 min.	20.00	215.00	WW	72,100
A Letter to Amy	C	1970	7 min.	20.00	140.00	WW	23
The Lion and the Mouse	C	1977	10 min.	40.00	250.00	CF	9
Little Blue and Little Yellow	C	1961	9 min.	19.00	180.00	MF	32
The Little Drummer Boy	C	1969	7 min.	20.00	140.00	WW	54
The Little Red Hen	C	----	10 min.	35.00	240.00	CF	78
The Little Rooster Who Made the Sun Rise	C	----	11 min.	40.00	255.00	CF	44
Louis James Hates School	C	1980	12 min.	----	----	LCA	40,92
Madeline	C	1955	7 min.	20.00	130.00	LCA	79
Madeline's Rescue	C	1959	7 min.	----	135.00	RF	7
Make Way for Ducklings	C	1955	11 min.	25.00	215.00	WW	27
Many Moons	C	1971	13 min.	20.00	185.00	MH	83,90
Meeting Strangers: Red Light, Green Light (Revised)	C	1984	19 min.	56.00	410.00	PF	84,93
Millions of Cats	B&W	1955	10 min.	15.00	195.00	WW	6
The Mole and the Christmas Tree	C	1977	6 min.	15.00	165.00	PF	54
The Mole in the Zoo	C	1973	10 min.	16.00	230.00	PF	100
Morris' Disappearing Bag	C	1982	6 min.	20.00	175.00	WW	12
The Most Wonderful Egg in the World	C	1987	6 min.	20.00	175.00	WW	83

TITLE	C or B&W	DATE	LENGTH	RENTAL	PRICE	PUBLISHER	NUMBER
Mother Duck & the Big Race	C	----	11 min	40.00	255.00	CF	20
The Mysterious Tadpole	C	1987	9 min.	20.00	215.00	WW	37,77
The Napping House	C	1987	5 min.	15.00	115.00	WW	15
Norman the Doorman	C	----	15 min.	25.00	255.00	WW	10
One Monday Morning	C	1972	10 min.	20.00	195.00	WW	65,83
Over in the Meadow	C	----	9 min.	20.00	175.00	WW	35
Owl and the Pussycat	C	1962	3 min.	10.00	85.00	WW	6,21,79
Peter's Chair	C	1971	6 min.	20.00	140.00	WW	49
A Picture for Harold's Room	C	1971	6 min.	20.00	175.00	WW	65
Pierre: A Cautionary Tale	C	----	6 min.	20.00	175.00	WW	64
A Pocket for Corduroy	C	1986	20 min.	70.00	485.00	PF	30,94
Puff, the Magic Dragon	C	----	24 min.	60.00	575.00	CF	38
The Pumpkin Who Couldn't Smile	C	----	23 min.	60.00	490.00	CF	58
Really Rosie	C	1975	26 min.	40.00	525.00	WW	35,36,73
Rosie's Walk	C	1970	5 min.	15.00	125.00	WW	44,64
The Selfish Giant	B&W	1972	14 min.	20.00	255.00	WW	52,70
The Shout It Out Alphabet Film	C	1969	12 min.	17.00	235.00	PF	2
The Shout It Out Numbers From 1 to 10	C	1982	6 min.	15.00	160.00	PF	35
Smile for Auntie	C	1979	5 min.	15.00	125.00	WW	14
The Sneetches	C	1974	13 min.	180.00	295.00	PF	40
The Snowman	C	1982	26 min.	40.00	525.00	WW	98
The Snowy Day	C	1964	6 min.	20.00	175.00	WW	89
The Sorcerer's Apprentice	C	1940	14 min.	20.00	275.00	WW	69
Stone Soup	C	1955	11 min.	25.00	215.00	WW	46
A Story, A Story	C	1974	10 min.	20.00	235.00	WW	47
Strega Nonna	C	----	9 min.	20.00	215.00	WW	69
Tale of the Groundhog's Shadow	C	1985	11 min.	40.00	255.00	CF	57
Teddy Bear's Ballon Trip	C	----	14 min.	40.00	320.00	CF	95
Teeny-Tiny and the Witch Woman	C	1980	14 min.	25.00	295.00	WW	99

TITLE	C or B&W	DATE	LENGTH	RENTAL	PRICE	PUBLISHER	NUMBER
The Twelve Days of Christmas	C	1972	6 min.	20.00	140.00	WW	54
The Ugly Duckling	C	1975	15 min.	25.00	315.00	WW	42
A Visit from St. Nicholas	C	----	4 min.	30.00	135.00	CF	54
Whistle for Willie	C	1965	6 min.	20.00	175.00	WW	7
Why Mosquitoes Buzz in People's Ears	C	1984	10 min.	20.00	235.00	WW	47,66
William's Doll	C	1981	18 min.	35.00	385.00	PF	94
Wynken, Blynken and Nod	C	1971	4 min.	15.00	115.00	WW	42
Yankee Doodle	C	1976	10 min.	20.00	195.00	WW	56
The Zax	C	1974	5 min.	25.00	130.00	PF	71

TITLE	C or B & W	DATE	LENGTH	PRICE	PUBLISHER	NUMBER
Alexander & the Windup Mouse (Leo Lionni's Caldecotts)	C	----	24 min.	29.95	MP	1,40,94
The Ant & the Dove	C	1962	8 min.	155.00	CP	66
Alligators All Around	C	----	2 min.	50.00	WW	2,80
The Amazing Bone	C	1986	11 min.	125.00	WW	69
Andy and the Lion	C	1955	10 min.	100.00	WW	9,28,68
Angus Lost	C	1982	11 min.	150.00	PF	7
Arthur's Christmas Cookies (Arthur Celebrates the Holidays)	C	----	40 min.	149.95	RH/MB	54
Arthur's Halloween (Arthur Celebrates the Holidays)	C	----	40 min.	149.95	RH/MB	58
Arthur's Thanksgiving (Arthur Celebrates the Holidays)	C	----	40 min.	149.95	RH/MB	61
The Bear and the Fly	C	1985	5 min.	65.00	WW	5
The Bear Who Slept Through Christmas	C	1983	60 min.	29.95	BT	54
Blueberries for Sal	C	----	9 min.	90.00	WW	5
A Boy, A Dog, and a Frog	C	1981	9 min.	145.00	PF	7,50
A Boy and a Boa	C	1975	13 min.	145.00	PF	81
The Bremen-Town Musicians	C	1981	11 min.	140.00	PF	73,76
The Camel Who Took a Walk	C	----	6 min.	70.00	WW	4
Caps for Sale	C	----	5 min.	60.00	WW	11,31,64
The Cat in the Hat (Dr. Seuss Showcase II)	C	----	51 min.	49.95	MP	6,31,97
Charlie Needs a Cloak	C	1976	8 min.	50.00	WW	30
Circus Baby	C	----	5 min.	60.00	WW	8,29,70
Cloudy With a Chance of Meatballs	C	----	15 min.	34.95	RH/MB	76,97
Corduroy	C	1985	16 min.	50.00	WW	30,40,94
Curious George	C	1983	83 min.	29.95	BT	11,26
Curious George Rides a Bike	C	----	10 min.	50.00	WW	18,29

TITLE	C or B & W	DATE	LENGTH	PRICE	PUBLISHER	NUMBER
Dorothy and the Ostrich	C	1982	9 min.	130.00	PF	19
Dr. DeSoto	C	1984	10 min.	50.00	WW	25
Draghetto	C	1979	12 min.	125.00	PF	26,38
Dragon Stew	C	1972	13 min.	180.00	BT	38,46
Dumbo	C	1951	63 min.	29.95	MP	8
The Elephant's Child	C	---	30 min.	29.95	MP	8
The Elves & the Shoemaker	C	---	6 min.	29.95	TA	59
The Emperor's New Clothes	C	1976	10 min.	135.00	PF	30,64,65,83
The First Easter Rabbit	C	1982	25 min.	250.00	CF	55
The Fisherman & His Wife	C	1977	20 min.	190.00	WW	55
Fish is Fish (5 Lionni Classics)	C	1987	30 min.	14.95	LL	45
The Five Chinese Brothers	C	---	10 min.	50.00	WW	48
Frederick (Leo Lionni's Caldecotts)	C	---	24 min.	49.95	MP	10
Frog and Toad are Friends: A Swim (Arnold Lobel Video Showcase)	C	---	60 min.	149.95	RH/MB	88,91
Frog and Toad are Friends: Spring (Arnold Lobel Video Showcase)	C	---	60 min.	149.95	RH/MB	87
Frog and Toad are Friends: The Story (Arnold Lobel Video Showcase)	C	---	60 min.	149.95	RH/MB	50
Frog and Toad Together: Dragons & Giants (Arnold Lobel Video Showcase)	C	---	60 min.	149.95	RH/MB	38,52
Frog and Toad Together: The Garden (Arnold Lobel Video Showcase)	C	---	60 min.	149.95	RH/MB	78
Frog Goes to Dinner	C	1985	12 min.	175.00	PF	46
The Frog Prince	C	---	6 min.	29.95	MP	50
The Frog Princess	C	1957	6 min.	130.00	CF	50
Frog Went A-Courtin'	C	---	12 min.	120.00	WW	50,73
Georgie	C	---	6 min.	70.00	WW	51,58

TITLE	C or B & W	DATE	LENGTH	PRICE	PUBLISHER	NUMBER
The Ghost with the Halloween Hicups	C	1985	7 min.	30.00	CF	51,58
The Giant Devil-Dingo	C	1985	10 min.	100.00	WW	52
The Gingerbread Boy	C	----	8 min.	29.95	TA	42
The Grasshopper & the Ants	C	1962	11 min.	195.00	CF	66
Green Eggs and Ham (The Cat in the Hat/ Dr. Seuss on the Loose)	C	1974	51 min.	37.95	LL	46
Hansel and Gretel	C	----	14 min.	29.95	RH/MB	99
Happy Birthday Moon	C	1986	7 min.	90.00	WW	23
Happy Lion's Treasure	C	----	9 min.	39.00	EBEC	9,100
Hanukkah	C	----	12 min.	39.00	EBEC	53
The Happy Owls	C	----	7 min.	90.00	WW	21,40
Harold and the Purple Crayon	C	----	8 min.	50.00	WW	13,32,64,65
Harold's Fairy Tale	C	1974	8 min.	100.00	WW	42
The Hat	C	----	6 min.	90.00	WW	31
Helpful Little Fireman	C	1966	11 min.	180.00	CF	26
Henny Penny	C	----	6 min.	29.95	TA	4,42, 44
Hercules	C	----	11 min.	110.00	WW	26
How the Trollusk Got His Hat (Mercer Mayer Stories)	C	----	30 min.	15.95	MP	31
How the Whale Got His Throat (Rudyard Kipling Classics)	C	----	25 min.	14.95	LL	45
How the Leopard Got His Spots (Just So Stories)	C	1985	30 min.	73.95	LL	47
Hush Little Baby	C	----	5 min.	60.00	WW	14
If I Ran the Zoo	C	----	18 min.	29.95	LL	100
In the Night Kitchen	C	----	6 min.	90.00	WW	65
Ira Sleeps Over	C	1977	15 min.	34.95	RH/MB	15,49,94
Jack and the Beanstalk	C	1977	10 min.	135.00	PP	52,78
Jonah and the Great Fish	C	1987	5 min.	70.00	WW	45
Ladybug, Ladybug, Winter is Coming	C	1976	10 min.	185.00	CF	CF
The Legend of Sleepy Hollow	C	----	49 min.	69.96	MP	51

TITLE	C or B & W	DATE	LENGTH	PRICE	PUBLISHER	NUMBER
Lentil	C	---	9 min.	90.00	WW	35,73,75
Leo On Vacation	C	1975	11 min.	135.00	PF	9
Leopold the See-Through Crumbpicker	C	1971	9 min.	50.00	WW	72,100
A Letter to Amy	C	1970	7 min.	70.00	WW	23,97
The Lion and the Mouse (Mr. Know it Owl's Video Tales: Aesop's Fables Vol. 1)	C	1986	30 min.	14.95	LL	9
The Little Drummer Boy	C	---	7 min.	50.00	WW	54
The Little Engine That Could	C	---	10 min.	185.00	CF	96
The Little Red Hen (Amye Rosenberg Stories)	C	---	30 min.	15.95	MP	19,44,78
The Little Red Lighthouse & the Great Gray Bridge	C	---	9 min.	90.00	WW	24
Little Red Riding Hood	C	1958	9 min.	130.00	PF	42,93
The Little Rooster Who Made the Sun Rise	C	1961	11 min.	180.00	CF	44
Little Tim & the Brave Sea Captain	C	---	11 min.	50.00	WW	24,85
The Lorax	C	1974	51 min.	37.95	LL	39,71
Lyle, Lyle Crocodile	C	---	30 min.	69.95	AV	80
Madeline	C	---	6 min.	29.95	RH/MB	62,79
Magic Fishbone	C	1982	11 min.	140.00	PF	69
Make Way for Ducklings	C	---	11 min.	50.00	WW	20,27
Meeting Strangers: Red Light, Green Light						
Mickey Mouse, The Brave Little Tailor (Cartoon Classics Collection Vol. 6)	C	1984	19 min.	250.00	PF	84,93
Millions of Cats	C	1987	25 min.	49.95	CF	10,52
The Mole and the Christmas Tree	B&W	---	10 min.	50.00	WW	6
The Mole in the Zoo	C	1977	6 min.	120.00	PF	54
Morris' Disappearing Bag	C	1977	10 min.	135.00	PF	100
	C	---	6 min.	50.00	WW	12,54

TITLE	C or B&W	DATE	LENGTH	PRICE	PUBLISHER	NUMBER
The Most Wonderful Egg in the World	C	1987	6 min.	90.00	WW	83
Mother Duck & the Big Race	C	----	11 min.	180.00	CF	20
The Mysterious Tadpole	C	1987	9 min.	110.00	WW	37,77
The Napping House	C	----	5 min.	60.00	WW	15
Norman the Doorman	C	----	15 min.	50.00	WW	10,13
One Monday Morning	C	1972	10 min.	100.00	WW	36,65,83
One Was Johnny	C	----	3 min.	50.00	WW	35
One Zillion Valentines	C	----	6 min.	29.95	RH/MB	60
Over in the Meadow	C	----	9 min.	90.00	WW	35
Owl and the Pussycat	C	----	7 min.	120.00	PF	6,21,79
Paddington Helps Out; Paddington Dines Out (Paddington Bear, Vol.2)	C	1985	50 min.	29.95	CF	5
Peter's Chair	C	1971	6 min.	70.00	WW	14,49
Pete's Dragon	C	----	105 min.	29.95	BC	38
Petunia	C	----	10 min.	50.00	WW	1
A Picture for Harold's Room	C	1971	6 min.	90.00	WW	13,65
Pierre: A Cautionary Tale	C	1985	50 min.	29.95	CF	5
A Pocket for Corduroy	C	1986	20 min.	320.00	PF	30,94
The Pokey Little Puppy (Best Loved Golden Books)	C	----	30 min.	15.95	MP	7
Puff, the Magic Dragon	C	----	45 min.	50.95	LL	38
The Pumpkin Who Couldn't Smile	C	----	23 min.	49.95	MP	58
Really Rosie	C	1975	26 min.	50.00	WW	35,36,73
Rosie's Walk	C	1970	5 min.	50.00	WW	44,64
Rumpelstiltskin	C	----	10 min.	29.95	RH/MB	42,69,74
The Saggy Baggy Elephant (Golden Jungle Animal Tales)	C	----	30 min.	15.95	MP	8
The Selfish Giant	B&W	1972	14 min.	130.00	WW	52,70
The Shout It Out Alphabet Film	C	1969	12 min.	135.00	PF	2
Shout It Out Numbers From 1 to 10	C	1982	6 min.	110.00	PF	35

TITLE	C or B & W	DATE	LENGTH	PRICE	PUBLISHER	NUMBER
Smile for Auntie	C	1979	5 min.	65.00	WW	14
The Sneetches (Cat in the Hat/Dr. Seuss on the Loose)	C	1974	51 min.	37.95	LL	40
The Snowman	C	1982	26 min.	50.00	WW	98
Snow White & the 7 Dwarfs	C	1983	60 min.	19.95	LL	59
The Snowy Day	C	----	6 min.	50.00	WW	89,98
The Sorcerer's Apprentice	C	----	14 min.	140.00	WW	69
Stone Soup	C	1974	11 min.	50.00	WW	46
A Story, A Story	C	----	10 min.	50.00	WW	47
The Story of Ping	C	----	10 min.	50.00	WW	20,48
The Story of Puss in Boots	C	----	89 min.	59.95	MP	6
Strega Nonna	C	----	9 min.	50.00	WW	69
Swimmy (Leo Lionni's Caldecotts)	C	----	24 min.	49.95	MP	45
Tale of The Groundhog's Shadow	C	1955	11 min.	140.00	CF	57
Tawny Scrawny Lion (Golden Jungle Animal Tales)	C	----	30 min.	15.95	MP	9
Teddy Bear's Balloon Trip	C	----	14 min.	225.00	CF	95
Teeny-Tiny and the Witch Woman	C	1980	14 min.	50.00	WW	99
The Three Little Pigs	C	----	8 min.	29.95	TA	4
Thumbelina	C	1977	9 min.	135.00	PF	34
Tikki Tikki Tembo	C	----	9 min.	50.00	WW	48,74
The Tortoise & the Hare	C	1986	30 min.	14.95	LL	12,82,91
The Twelve Days of Christmas	C	1972	6 min.	70.00	WW	54
The Ugly Duckling	C	1985	30 min.	19.95	LL	19,20,42
A Visit from St. Nicholas	C	1949	4 min.	105.00	CP	54
Where the Wild Things Are	C	----	8 min.	50.00	WW	65,72
Whistle for Willie	C	----	6 min.	90.00	WW	7
Why Mosquitoes Buzz in People's Ears	C	1985	10 min.	50.00	WW	47,66
Winnie the Pooh and the Blustery Day	C	----	25 min.	19.95	MP	86

TITLE	C or B & W	DATE	LENGTH	PRICE	PUBLISHER	NUMBER
Winnie the Pooh & Tigger, Too!	C	----	25 min.	19.95	MP	5
Winnie the Witch & the Frightened Ghost (Fran Allison's Autumn Tales of Winnie the Witch)						
Wynken, Blynken and Nod	C	----	25 min.	69.00	SVE	51
Yankee Doodle	C	1971	4 min.	60.00	WW	42
The Zax	C	1976	10 min.	100.00	WW	56
(Cat in the Hat/Dr. Seuss on the Loose)	C	1974	51 min.	37.95	LL	71

Bibliography

Aarons, Trudy and Francine Koelsch. *101 Easy Art Activities*. Tucson, Ariz.: Communication Skills Builders, 1985; 151 pp., $19.95.

Adams, Adrienne. *The Easter Egg Artists*. New York: MacMillan, 1976; 32 pp., $12.95.

——. *The Great Valentine's Day Balloon Race*. New York: MacMillan, 1986; 32 pp., $10.95.

Adelson, Leone. *All Ready for School*. New York: McKay, 1957; 24 pp., $2.75.

——. *Who Blew That Whistle?*. New York: R. Scott, 1946; 45 pp., $1.25.

Adler, David. *A Picture Book of Hannukah*. New York: Holiday House, Inc., 1982; 32 pp., $12.95.

Aesop. *The Lion and the Mouse*. Mahwah, N.J.: Troll Associates, 1981; 32 pp., $9.79.

Aleichem, Sholom. *Hannukah Money*. New York: Greenwillow, 1978; 32 pp., $11.75.

Alexander, Martha. *How My Library Grew*. Bronx, N.Y.: Wilson, 1983; 32 pp., $15.00.

——. *No Ducks in Our Bathtub*. New York: Dial Books for the Young, 1973; 32 pp., $8.95.

——. *Sabrina*. New York: Dial Press, 1971; 28 pp., $5.95.

Allard, Harry. *Bumps in the Night*. New York: Bantam Books, 1987; 48 pp., $2.25 pb.

——. *It's So Nice to Have a Wolf Around the House*. New York: Doubleday, 1977; 28 pp., $8.95.

——. *Miss Nelson Has a Field Day*. Boston: Houghton Mifflin Co., 1985: 32 pp., $12.95.

Allen, Pamela. *Who Sank the Boat?* New York: Putnam Publishing Group, 1983; 32 pp., $10.95.

Andersen, H.C. *The Princess and the Pea*. Boston: Houghton Mifflin Co., 1978; 32 pp., $10.95.

Arnstein, Helen. *Billy and Our New Baby*. New York: Human Sciences Press, Inc., 1973; 32 pp., $13.95.

Asbjornsen, Peter. *The Three Billy Boats Gruff*. San Diego, Calif.: Harcourt, Brace Jovanovich, Inc., 1957; 28 pp., $10.95.

Asch, Frank. *Bread and Honey*. New York: Parents Magazine Press, 1982; 48 pp., $5.95.

——. *Moon Bear*. New York: Charles Scribner's Sons, 1978; 28 pp., $8.95.

——. *Popcorn*. New York: Parents Magazine Press, 1979; 48 pp., $5.95.

——. *Sand Cake*. New York: Parents Magazine Press, 1979; 48 pp., $5.95.

——. *Starbaby*. New York: Charles Scribner's Sons, 1980; 28 pp., $9.95.

——. *Turtle Tale*. New York: Dial Books for the Young, 1980; 32 pp., $2.75 pb.

Ayer, Jacqueline. *Nu Dang and His Kite.* San Diego, Calif.: Harcourt, Brace Jovanovich, Inc., 1959; 30 pp., $3.49.

Balian, Lorna. *Humbug Potion.* Nashville, Tenn.: Abingdon, 1984; 28 pp., $12.95.

———. *Humbug Rabbit.* Nashville, Tenn.: Abingdon, 1974; 32 pp., $12.95.

———. *Humbug Witch.* Nashville, Tenn.: Abingdon, 1965; 32 pp., $10.95.

———. *Leprechauns Never Lie.* Nashville, Tenn.: Abingdon, 1980; 32 pp., $8.95.

———. *Sometimes It's Turkey.* Nashville, Tenn.: Abingdon, 1986; 32 pp., $10.95.

Banchek, Linda. *Snake In. Snake Out.* San Diego, Calif.: Harcourt, Brace Jovanovich, Inc., 1978; 29 pp., $11.89.

Bang, Molly. *Ten, Nine, Eight.* New York: Greenwillow Books, 1983; 24 pp., $11.95.

Barlin, Anne and Paul. *Dance-A-Folk Song.* New York: Bowmar Publishing Corp., 1974; 96 pp., $14.95.

Barrett, John. *The Easter Bear.* Chicago: Children's Press, 1981; 32 pp., $11.27.

Barrett, Judi. *Animals Should Definitely Not Wear Clothing.* New York: MacMillan, 1970; 32 pp., $12.95.

———. *Benjamin's 365 Birthdays.* New York: MacMillan, 1978; 34 pp., $4.95 pb.

———. *Cloudy with a Chance of Meatballs.* New York: MacMillan, 1978; 30 pp., $13.95.

———. *I'm Too Small, You're Too Big.* New York: Atheneum, 1981; 31 pp., $9.95.

Bauer, Caroline Feller. *This Way to Books.* New York: H.W. Wilson Co., 1983; 363 pp., $30.00

———. *Too Many Books!.* New York: Frederick Warne & Co., Inc., 1984; 32 pp., $11.95.

Baum, Arline. *One Bright Monday Morning.* New York: Random House, 1962; 34 pp., $4.99.

Beatty, Hetty. *Little Owl Indian.* Boston: Houghton Mifflin Co., 1951; 32 pp., $4.23.

Becker, Joyce. *Hanukkah Crafts.* New York: Bonim Books, 1978; 144 pp., $6.95.

Beim, Jerrole. *The Swimming Hole.* New York: Morrow, 1950; unpaged, $3.78.

Bell, Barbara, ed. *Highlights Magazine for Children.* April 1984; $2.25.

Bemelmans, Ludwig. *Madeline's Rescue.* New York: Viking Press, 1939. 56 pp., $13.95.

———. *Rosebud.* New York: Random House, 1942; 32 pp. (no price).

Benchley, Nathaniel. *A Ghost Named Fred.* New York: Harper & Row, 1968; 64 pp., $10.89.

———. *The Magic Sled.* New York: Harper & Row, 1972; 64 pp., $11.89.

———. *Red Fox and His Canoe.* New York: Harper & Row, 1964; 64 pp., $10.89

Benjamin, Alan. *Ribtickle Town.* New York: MacMillan, 1983; unpaged, $10.95.

Bently, Anne. *The Groggs' Day Out.* New York: Deutsch, 1981; 33 pp., $9.95.

Benton, Robert. *Don't Ever Wish for a 7 Ft. Bear.* New York: Knopf, 1972; 34 pp., $5.99.

Berenstain, Stan. *The Berenstain Bears Go to Camp.* New York: Random House, 1978; 32 pp., $3.99.

———. *The Berenstein Bears Visit the Dentist.* New York: Random House, 1981; 32 pp., $4.99.

Berenstain, Stan and Jan Berenstain. *The Bike Lesson.* New York: Random House, 1964; 64 pp., $6.99.

Berson, Howard. *Joseph and the Snake.* New York: MacMillan, 1979; unpaged, $6.95.

Bester, Roger. *Fireman Jim.* New York: Crown, 1981; 32 pp., $9.95.

———. *Big and Easy Art.* Calif.: Teacher Created Materials, Inc., 1986; 32 pp., $1.95.

Bishop, Claire. *Twenty-two Bears.* New York: Viking Press, 1964; 31 pp., no price.

Blegvad, Lenore. *The Great Hamster Hunt*. San Diego, Calif.: Harcourt, Brace Jovanovich, Inc., 1969; 32 pp., $2.97.

Blos, Joan. *Martin's Hats*. New York: Morrow, 1984; 32 pp., $10.88.

Boegehold, Betty. *You Can Say "No"*. New York: Golden/Western, 1985; 23 pp., $4.95.

Bonsall, Crosby. *Mine's the Best*. New York: Harper & Row Junior Books, 1973; 32 pp., $9.89.

Bornstein, Ruth. *Indian Bunny*. Chicago: Children's Press, 1973; unpaged, $4.33.

Breinburg, Petronella. *Shawn's Red Bike*. New York: Crowell, 1975; 24 pp., $6.95.

Bridwell, Norman. *Clifford's Good Deeds*. New York: Scholastic, Inc., 1985; 32 pp., $1.95.

Bright, Robert. *Georgie and the Magician*. New York: Doubleday, 1966; 45 pp., $2.50 pb.

——. *Georgie and the Runaway Balloon*. New York: Doubleday, 1983; 32 pp., $3.95.

——. *Georgie's Halloween*. New York: Doubleday, 1958; 30 pp., $4.95.

——. *Which Is Willy?* New York: Doubleday, 1962; unpaged, no price.

Browne, Anthony. *Bear Hunt*. New York: Atheneum, 1980; 24 pp., $8.95.

Brown, David. *Someone Always Needs a Policeman*. New York: Simon and Schuster, 1972; 40 pp., $3.95.

Brown, Marc. *Arthur Goes to Camp*. Boston; Little, Brown & Co., 1982; 32 pp., $14.95.

——. *Hand Rhymes*. New York: E.P. Dutton, 1983; 32 pp., $11.95.

——. *Perfect Pigs: An Introduction to Manners*. Boston: Little, Brown & Co., 1983; 29 pp., $12.45.

Brown, Margaret Wise. *Big Red Barn*. New York: Harper & Row Junior Books, 1965; 13 pp., $8.70.

——. *Goodnight, Moon*. New York: Harper & Row Junior Books, 1947; 30 pp., $8.89.

——. *The Little Fireman*. New York: Harper & Row Junior Books, 1952; 34 pp., $9.70.

——. *Red Light! Green Light!* New York: Doubleday, 1944; unpaged, $5.95.

——. *The Seashore Noisy Book*. Reading, Mass.: Addison-Wesley, 1941; 40 pp., $10.89.

——. *The Sleepy Little Lion*. New York: Harper & Row Junior Books, 1947; 24 pp., $12.89.

——. *The Summer Noisy Book*. New York: Harper & Row, 1951; 40 pp., $10.89.

——. *Winter Noisy Book*. New York: Harper & Row, 1947; 40 pp., $10.89.

Brunhoff, Laurent de. *Babar and the Ghost*. New York: Random House, 1981; 34 pp., $6.99.

Brustlein, Janice. *Little Bear Marches in the St. Patrick's Day Parade*. New York: Lothrop, Lee & Shepard, 1967; 26 pp., $3.50.

Bulla, Clyde. *Daniel's Duck*. New York: Harper & Row Junior Books, 1979; 64 pp., $10.89.

Bunting, Eve. *The Valentine Bears*. Boston: Harper & Row Junior Books, 1976; 16 pp., $11.89.

Burton, Virginia. *Katy and the Big Snow*. Boston: Houghton Mifflin Co., 1943; 40 pp., $11.95.

Byars, Betsy. *Go and Hush the Baby*. New York: Viking Penguin, Inc., 1971; 30 pp., $11.95.

Calhoun, Mary. *Hot Air Henry*. New York: William Morrow, 1981; 40 pp., $10.89.

——. *The Hungry Leprechaun*. New York: William Morrow, 1962; 28 pp., $11.88.

Cameron, Ann. *Harry (the Monster)*. New York: Pantheon Books, 1980; 36 pp., $6.99.

Cameron, Polli. *"I Can't," Said the Ant*. New York: Coward, 1961; unpaged., $7.99.

Caney, Steven. *Steven Caney's Toy Book*. New York: Workman Publishing Co.: 1972; 176 pp., $8.95.

Canfield, Jane. *The Frog Prince*. New York: Harper & Row, 1970; 31 pp., $4.79.

Cantieni, Benita. *Little Elephant and Big Mouse*. Natick, Mass.: Picture Book Studios USA, 1981; 32 pp., $13.95.

Carle, Eric. *Do You Want to Be My Friend?*. New York: Harper & Row Junior Books, 1971; 31 pp., $12.89.

———. *Have You Seen My Cat?*. Natick, Mass.: Picture Book Studios USA, 1987; 21 pp., $14.95.

———. *The Mixed-Up Chameleon*. New York: Harper & Row Junior Books, 1984; 32 pp., $13.89.

———. *Secret Birthday Message*. New York: Harper & Row Junior Books, 1972; 24 pp., $12.89.

———. *The Tiny Seed*. Natick, Mass.: Picture Book Studio USA, 1987; 32 pp., $12.95.

———. *The Very Hungry Caterpillar*. New York: Putnam Publishing Group, 1986; 32 pp., $12.95.

Cave, Peter L. *500 Games*. New York: Grossett and Dunlap, 1973; 160 pp., $1.95.

Chardiet, Bernice. *C is for Circus*. New York: Walker & Co., 1971; unpaged., $5.85.

———. *Charlie Brown's Super Book of Things to Do and Collect*. New York: Random House, 1975; 80 pp., $5.99.

Chase, Catherine. *The Mouse in My House*. Elgin, Ill.: Dandelion, 1979; unpaged., $2.50.

Chernoff, Goldie Taub. *Just a Box?*. New York: Walker & Co., 1973; 23 pp., $1.75 pb.

Chesler, Bernice. *Do a Zoom-Do*. Boston: Little Brown & Co., 1975; 118 pp., $7.95.

Chlad, Dorothy. *Matches, Lighters and Firecrackers are Not Toys*. Chicago: Children's Press, 1982; 31 pp., $11.00.

———. *Strangers*. Chicago: Children's Press, 1982; 31 pp., $11.00.

Choate, Judith, and Jane Green. *Scrapcraft: 50 Easy to Make Handicraft Projects*. New York: Doubleday, 1973; 64 pp., $4.95.

Christelow, Eileen. *Jerome the Babysitter*. Boston: Houghton Mifflin Co., 1985; 32 pp., $12.95.

Clifton, Lucille. *Three Wishes*. New York: Viking Penguin, Inc., 1974; 26 pp., $6.95.

Cophen, Carol. *Wake Up, Groundhog!*. New York: Crown Publications, Inc., 1975; 31 pp., $4.95.

Cohen, Miriam. *Bee My Valentine!*. New York: Greenwillow, 1978; 32 pp., $11.88.

———. *The New Teacher*. New York: MacMillan, 1972; 31 pp., $3.95.

Cole, Ann; Carolyn Haas; Faith Bushness; and Betty Weinberger. *I Saw a Purple Cow and 100 Other Recipes for Learning*. Boston: Little, Brown & Co., 1972; 96 pp., $14.45.

Cole, Ann; Carolyn Haas, Elizabeth Heller, and Betty Weinberger. *A Pumpkin in a Pear Tree*. Boston: Little, Brown & Co., 1976; 112 pp., $14.45.

Cole, Ann; Carolyn Haas; and Betty Weinberger. *Purple Cow to the Rescue*. Boston: Little, Brown & Co.: 1982; 160 pp., $14.45.

Cole, Joanna. *A Fish Hatches*. New York: Morrow, 1978; 39 pp., $11.88.

Cole, William. *Frances, Face-Maker*. Cleveland, Ohio: William Collins, 1963; unpaged, $3.41.

Coleman, Satis N., and Alice G. Thom. *Singing Time: A Book of Songs for Little Children*. New York: The John Day Co., 1928; 48 pp., $3.50.

Condit, Martha Olson. *Something to Make, Something to Think About*. New York: Four Winds, 1975; 39 pp., $4.95.

Coville, Bruce. *The Foolish Giant*. New York: Harper & Row Junior Books, 1978; 46 pp., $10.89.

Cressey, James. *Max the Mouse*. Englewood Cliffs, N.J.: Prentice-Hall, 1977; unpaged, $4.95.

Crews, Donald. *Harbor*. New York: Greenwillow, 1982; 32 pp., $11.88.

——. *Ten Black Dots*. New York: Greenwillow, 1986; 32 pp., $11.88.

Cromwell, Liz, and Dixie Hibner, and John R. Faitel. *Finger Frolics—Revised*. Mount Rainier, Md.: Gryphon House, 1983; 83 pp., $14.95.

Dabcovick, Lydia. *Sleepy Bear*. New York: E.P. Duton, 1982; 32 pp., $9.95 pb.

Davidson, Amanda. *Teddy At the Seashore*. New York: H. Holt & Co., 1984; 24 pp., $7.95.

——. *Teddy's First Christmas*. New York: H. Holt & Co., 1982; 24 pp., $7.95.

Davis, Gibbs. *The Other Emily*. Boston: Houghton Mifflin Co. , 1984; 32 pp., $10.95.

DeGroat, Diane. *Alligator's Toothache*. New York: Crown, 1977, 30 pp., $4.95.

Delamar, Gloria T. *Children's Counting-Out Rhymes, Fingerplays, Jump-Rope and Bounce-Ball Chants and other Rhythms*. Jefferson, N.C.: McFarland & Co., Inc., 1983; 206 pp., $19.95.

Delaney, M.C. *The Marigold Monster*. New York: E.P. Dutton, 1983; 32 pp., $9.95.

Delton, Judy. *Groundhog's Day at the Doctor*. New York: Parents Magazine Press, 1981; 48 pp., $5.95.

——. *Penny Wise, Fun Foolish*. New York: Crown Publications, Inc., 1977; 48 pp., $6.95.

——. *A Pet for Duck and Bear*. New York: Albert Whitman & Co., 1982; 32 pp., $10.25.

dePaola, Tomie. *Andy (That's My Name)*. New York: Prentice-Hall Press, 1973; 30 pp., $9.95.

——. *Big Anthony and the Magic Ring*. San Diego, Calif.: Harcourt, Brace Jovanovich, Inc., 1987; 32 pp., $12.95.

——. *Fin M'Coul*. New York: Holiday House, 1981; 29 pp., $12.95.

——. *The Legend of Blue Bonnet*. New York: Putnam Publishing Group, 1983; 29 pp., $10.95.

deRegniers, Beatrice. *May I Bring a Friend?*. New York: MacMillan, 1964; 44 pp., $12.95.

——. *The Shadow Book*. San Diego, Calif.: Harcourt, Brace Jovanovich, Inc., 1960; 27 pp., $5.95.

Disney, Walt. *The Walt Disney Song Book*. New York: Golden Press, 1977; 93 pp., $6.95.

Domanska, Janina. *The Turnip*. New York: MacMillan, 1969; 29 pp., $5.95.

Dragonwagon, Crescent. *Wind Rose*. New York: Harper & Row, 1976; 30 pp., $9.57.

Duke, Kate. *Seven Froggies Went to School*. New York: E.P. Dutton, 1985; 32 pp., $11.95.

Duvoisin, Roger. *Crocus*. New York: Alfred A. Knopf, 1977; 28 pp., $6.99.

——. *The Happy Hunter*. New York: Lothrop, Lee & Shepard Books, 1961; 31 pp., $2.83.

——. *Periwinkle*. New York: Alfred A. Knopf, 1976; 28 pp., $5.99.

——. *Petunia and the Song*. New York: Alfred A. Knopf, 1951; 31 pp., $3.49.

——. *Petunia's Christmas*. New York: Alfred A. Knopf, 1963; 28 pp., $8.99.

——. *Veronica and the Birthday Present*. New York: Alfred A. Knopf, 1971; 28 pp., $8.99.

Elliott, Dan. *Ernie's Little Lie*. New York: Random House, 1983; 40 pp., $6.99.

——. *A Visit to the Sesame Street Firehouse*. New York: Random House, 1983; 32 pp., $4.99.

Etkin, Ruth. *The Rhythm Band Book*. New York: Sterling Publishing Co., Inc., 1978; 96 pp., $6.69.

Farber, Norma. *Never Say Ugh to a Bug*. New York: Greenwillow, 1979; 32 pp., $11.88.

Fatio, Louise. *The Happy Lion*. New York: McGraw-Hill, 1964; 32 pp., $10.95.

——. *The Happy Lion in Africa*. New York: McGraw-Hill, 1955; 28 pp., $10.95.

——. *Hector Penguin*. New York: McGraw-Hill, 1973; 29 pp., $6.84.

Feder, Paula. *Where Does the Teacher Live?*. New York: E.P. Dutton, 1979; 48 pp., $7.95.

Fiarotta, Phyllis. *Snips and Snails and Walnut Whales*. New York: Workman Publishing Co., Inc., 1975; 288 pp., $8.95.

——. *Sticks and Stones and Ice Cream Cones*. New York: Workman Publishng Co., 1973; 322 pp., $8.95.

Fiarotta, Phyllis and Noel Fiarotta. *Be What You Want To Be!: The Complete Dress-Up and Pretend Craft Book*. New YorkWorkman Publishing Co; 1977; 304 pp., $5.95.

——. *Confetti: The Kid's Make-It-Yourself, Do-It-Yourself Party Book*. New York: Workman Publishing Co., 1978; 224 pp., $10.95.

——. *Pin It, Tack It, Hang It*. New York: Workman Publishing Co., 1975; 283 pp., $9.95.

Fisher, Aileen Lucia. *Where Does Everyone Go?*. New York: Crowell, 1961; 30 pp., $3.95.

Flack, Marjorie. *Ask Mr. Bear*. New York: MacMillan, 1986; 32 pp., $3.95 pb.

Flora, James. *Leopold, The Sea-Through Crumbpicker*. San Diego, Calif.: Harcourt, Brace Jovanovich, Inc., 1961; 29 pp., $5.95.

Forte, Imogene. *The Kid's Stuff Book of Patterns, Projects and Plans*. Nashville, Tenn.: Incentive Publishing, Inc., 1982; 199 pp., $12.95.

Freeman, Don. *Bearymore*. New York: Viking Penguin, Inc., 1976; 40 pp., $12.50.

——. *The Chalk Box Story*. Philadelphia, Penn.: J.B. Lippincott, 1976; 38 pp., $7.95.

——. *Quiet! There's a Canary in the Library*. Chicago: Children's Press, 1969; 48 pp., $10.60.

——. *Space Witch*. New York: Viking Penguin, Inc., 1979; 48 pp., $3.95.

Freeman, Jean. *Cynthia and the Unicorn*. New York: W.W. Norton, 1967; unpaged., no price.

Fuchshuber, Annegert. *The Wishing Hat*. New York: William Morrow, 1977; 28 pp., $5.95.

Gackenbach, Dick. *Annie and the Mud Monster*. New York: Lothrop, Lee and Shepard, 1982; 29 pp., $8.59.

——. *Claude and Pepper*. Boston: Houghton Mifflin Co., 1974; 32 pp., $10.95.

——. *Harry and the Terrible Whatzit*. Boston: Houghton Mifflin Co., 1978; 32 pp., $12.95.

——. *Hattie Be Quiet, Hattie Be Good.* New York: Harper & Row Junior Books, 1977; 32 pp., $9.89.

——. *The Perfect Mouse.* New York: MacMillan, 1984; 32 pp., $10.95.

——. *Poppy the Panda.* Boston: Houghton Mifflin Co., 1984; 32 pp., $11.95.

Gag, Wanda. *The Funny Thing.* New York: Putnam Publishing Group, 1960; unpaged, $6.99.

——. *Millions of Cats.* New York: Putnam Publishing Group, 1977; 112 pp., $7.95.

Galdone, Paul. *The Gingerbread Boy.* Boston: Houghton Mifflin Co., 1975; 40 pp., $12.95.

——. *Little Red Riding Hood.* New York: McGraw-Hill, 1974; 32 pp., $14.95.

——. *The Magic Porridge Pot.* Boston: Houghton Mifflin Co., 1972; 32 pp., $11.95.

——. *The Three Little Pigs.* Boston: Houghton Mifflin Co., 1970; 32 pp., $12.95.

Gannett, Ruth. *Katie and the Sad Noise.* New York: Random House, 1961; 62 pp., $2.39.

Geisel, Theodor. *The 500 Hats of Bartholomew Cubbins.* New York: Vanguard Press, Inc., 1938; 44 pp., $7.95.

Gerstein, Mordicai. *Arnold of the Ducks.* New York: Harper & Row Junior Books, 1983; 64 pp., $12.89.

——. *Roll Over!.* New York: Crown Publishers, 1984; 32 pp., $7.95.

Gibbons, Gail. *Fire! Fire!.* New York: Harper & Row Junior Books, 1984; 40 pp., $10.89.

——. *Thanksgiving Day.* New York: Holiday House, Inc., 1983; 32 pp., $12.95.

Gilbreath, Alice. *Beginning Crafts for Beginning Readers.* Chicago: Follett Publishing Co., 1972; 32 pp., $5.97.

——. *Making Toys That Crawl and Slide.* Chicago: Follet Publishing Co., 1978; 32 pp., $5.97.

——. *More Beginning Crafts for Beginning Readers.* Chicago: Follett Publishing Co., 1976; 32 pp., $5.97.

Glazer, Tom. *Do Your Ears Hang Low?.* New York: Doubleday and Co., Inc., 1980; 96 pp., $12.95.

——. *Eye Winker, Tom Tinker, Chin Chopper.* New York: Doubleday and Co., Inc., 1973; 91 pp., $10.95.

——. *Music for Ones and Twos.* New York: Doubleday and Co., Inc., 1983; 96 pp., $7.95.

Goffstein, M.B. *Fish for Supper.* New York: Dial Books for the Young, 1976; 32 pp., $5.89.

——. *Laughing Latkes.* New York: Farrar, Straus & Giroux, Inc., 1980; 32 pp., $6.95.

Graham, Al. *Timothy Turtle.* San Diego, Calif.: Harcourt, Brace Jovanovich, Inc., 1940; 28 pp., $5.95.

Graham, Margaret. *Benjy's Boat Trip.* New York: Harper & Row Junior Books, 1977; 30 pp., $13.89.

Greenberg, Barbara. *The Bravest Babysitter.* New York: Dial Books for the Young, 1977; 32 pp., $6.46.

Greene, Ellin. *The Pumpkin Giant.* New York: Lothrop, Lee & Shepard Books, 1970; 40 pp., (no price).

Greene, Graham. *The Little Train.* New York: Doubleday and Co., Inc., 1973; 42 pp., $5.95.

Greydanus, Rose. *Animals at the Zoo.* Mahwah, N.J.: Troll Associates, 1980; 32 pp., $5.41.

Grimm, Jacob. *Rumplestiltskin.* New York: Holiday House, Inc., 1983; 32 pp., $10.95.

Grimm, Jacob et al. *Snow White and the Seven Dwarfs.* Natick, Mass.: Picture Book Studio USA, 1985; 40 pp., $13.95.

Guy, Rose. *Mother Crocodile.* New York: Delacorte Press, 1981; 32 pp., $10.95.

Hamsa, Bobbie. *Your Pet Penguin.* Chicago: Children's Press, 1980; 32 pp., $10.60.

Harrop, Beatrice. *Sing Hey Diddle Diddle.* London: A & C Black Ltd., 1983; 66 pp., $9.95.

Hart, Jane. *Singing Bee!: A Collection of Favorite Children's Songs.* New York: Lothrop, Lee and Shepard Books, 1982; 160 pp., $17.95.

Hautzig, Deborah. *A Visit to the Sesame Street Library.* New York: Random House, 1986; 32 pp., $4.99.

———. *A Visit to the Sesame Street Hospital.* New York: Random House, 1985; 32 pp., $4.99.

Hawes, Judy. *Ladybug, Ladybug, Fly Away Home.* New York: Harper & Row, 1967; 32 pp., $10.89.

Hazell, Bee Gee. *Paper Plate Animals.* New York: Instructo/McGraw-Hill, 1982; 22 pp., $3.95.

Hazen, Barbara. *The Me I See!* Nashville, Tenn.: Abingdon, 1978; unpaged., $5.21.

Hill, Eric. *Good Morning, Baby Bear.* New York: Random House, 1984; 24 pp., $4.99.

Hillert, Margaret. *The Three Bears.* Cleveland, Ohio: Modern Curriculum Press, 1963; 32 pp., $4.39.

Hirsch, Marilyn. *I Love Hanukkah.* New York: Holiday House, 1984; 32 pp., $12.95.

———. *Potatoe Pancakes All Around.* Philadelphia: Jewish Publications Society, 1982; 34 pp., $5.95 pb.

Hoban, Lillian. *Arthur's Honey Bear.* New York: Harper & Row Junior Books, 1974; 64 pp., $10.89.

———. *Turtle Spring.* New York: Greenwillow, 1978; 47 pp., $5.49.

Hogan, Russell. *A Baby Sitter for Frances.* New York: Harper & Row Junior Books, 1964; 28 pp., $11.89.

———. *A Bargain for Frances.* New York: Harper & Row Junior Books, 1970; 64 pp., $10.89.

———. *Dinner at Alberta's.* New York: Harper & Row Junior Books, 1975; 40 pp., $11.89.

Hoban, Tana. *Circles, Triangles and Squares.* New York: MacMillan, 1974; 32 pp., $11.95.

———. *Is it Red? Is it Yellow? Is it Blue?.* New York: Greenwillow, 1978; 32 pp., $11.75.

Hoff, Sydney. *Grizzwold.* New York: Harper & Row Junior Books, 1963; 64 pp., $10.89.

Hoff, Syd. *Henrietta, Circus Star.* Easton, Md.: Garrard Publishng Co., 1978; 32 pp., $6.69.

———. *Henrietta's Fourth of July.* Easton, Md.: Garrard Publishing Co., 1981; 32 pp., $6.69.

———. *The Littlest Leaguer.* Old Tappan, N.J.: Windmill Books, 1976; 48 pp., $2.50 pb.

———. *Oliver.* New York: Harper & Row Junior Books, 1960; 64 pp., $10.89.

———. *Sammy the Seal.* New York: Harper & Row Junior Books, 1959; 64 pp., $10.89.

———. *Slithers.* New York: Putnam Publishers, 1968; 48 pp., $4.97.

———. *When Will it Snow?.* New York: Harper & Row Junior Books, 1971; 32 pp., $11.89.

Hogrogian, Nonny. *Carrot Cake.* New York: Greenwillow, 1977; 27 pp., $10.51.

Hogstrom, Daphne. *Little Boy Blue: Finger Plays for Old and New.* Wisc.: Golden Press, 1966; 23 pp., $3.95.

Hoguet, Susan. *I Unpacked My Grandmother's Trunk.* New York: E.P. Dutton, 1983; 58 pp., $10.95.

Holl, Adelaide. *The Rain Puddle.* New York: Lothrop, Lee and Shepard Books, 1965; 64 pp., $11.88.

Howe, Caroline. *Counting Penguins.* New York: Harper & Row Junior Books, 1983; 32 pp., $11.89.

Howe, James. *The Day the Teacher Went Bananas.* New York: E.P. Dutton, 1984; 32 pp., $10.95.

Hughes, Peter. *The Emperor's Oblong Pancake.* New York: Abelard-Schuman, 1961; unpaged., (no price).

Hurd, Edith. *Johnny Lion's Book.* New York: Harper & Row Junior Books, 1965; 64 pp., $10.89.

———. *Last One Home Is a Green Pig.* New York: Harper & Row Junior Books, 1959; 64 pp., $10.89.

———. *Starfish.* New York: Harper & Row Junior Books, 1962; 32 pp., $12.89.

Hurd, Thatcher. *Mama Don't Allow.* New York: Harper & Row Junior Books, 1984; 40 pp., $12.89.

Hutchins, Pat. *Happy Birthday, Sam.* New York: Greenwillow, 1978; 32 pp., $11.88.

———. *King Henry's Palace.* New York: Greenwillow, 1983; 56 pp., $10.25.

———. *Instructor's Artfully Easy!.* New York: Instructor's Books, 1983; 160 pp., $15.95.

Ipcar, Dahlov. *The Biggest Fish in the Sea.* New York: Viking Penguin, Inc., 1972; unpaged., $4.95.

Isadora, Rachel. *Ben's Trumpet.* New York: Greenwillow, 1979; 32 pp., $13.00.

Isele, Elizabeth. *The Frog Princess: A Russian Tale Retold.* New York: Harper & Row Junior Books, 1984; 32 pp., $11.89.

Iwamura, Kazuo. *Tan Tan's Hat.* New York: Bradbury Press, 1983; 40 pp., $7.95.

Janice. *Little Bear's Christmas.* New York: Lothrop, Lee and Shepard Books, 1964; 26 pp., $10.88.

———. *Little Bear's Pancake Party.* New York: Lothrop, Lee and Shepard Books, 1960; 34 pp., $10.88.

———. *Little Bear's Thanksgiving.* New York. Lothrop, Lee and Shepard Books. 1981; 64 pp., $2.50 pb.

———. *Harold's Trip to the Sky.* New York: Harper & Row Junior Books, 1957; 64 pp., $10.89.

Johnson, Mildred. *Wait, Skates!.* Chicago: Children's Press, 1982; 32 pp., $9.27.

Joyce, Irma. *Never Talk to Strangers.* New York: Western Publishing Co., Inc., 1985; 32 pp., $4.95.

Kahl, Virginia. *The Habits of Rabbits.* New York: Charles Scribner's Sons, 1957; 32 pp., $5.99.

Kalan, Robert. *Jump, Frog, Jump.* New York: Greenwillow, 1981; 32 pp., $11.88.

Keats, Ezra Jack. *Jennie's Hat.* New York: Harper & Row Junior Books, 1966; 34 pp., $12.89.

———. *Kitten for a Day.* New York: Harper & Row Junior Books, 1968; 32 pp., $12.89.

———. *My Dog is Lost!.* New York: Crowell, 1960; 39 pp., $3.50.

———. *Pet Show.* New York: MacMillan, 1972; 32 pp., $14.95.

——. *Regards to the Man in the Moon.* New York: MacMillan, 1987; 32 pp., $12.95.

——. *The Trip.* New York: William Morrow, 1978; 32 pp., $3.95.

——. *Whistle for Willie.* New York: Viking Penguin, Inc., 1964; 32 pp., $11.95.

Keller, Charles. *Glory, Glory, How Peculiar.* New York: Prentice-Hall, Inc., 1967; 32 pp., $4.95.

Keller, Holly. *Geraldine's Blanket.* New York: Greenwillow, 1984; 32 pp., $11.88.

——. *Will It Rain?.* New York: Greenwillow, 1984; 24 pp., $10.88.

Kellogg, Steven. *The Mysterious Tadpole.* New York: Dial Books for the Young, 1977; 32 pp., $11.89.

Kennedy, Richard. *The Leprechaun's Story.* New York: E.P. Dutton, 1979; 37 pp., $11.50.

Kent, Jack. *The Biggest Shadow in the Zoo.* New York: Parents Magazine Press, 1981; 48 pp., $5.95.

——. *Clotilda.* New York: Random House, 1978; 36 pp., $1.95 pb.

——. *The Fat Cat.* New York: Scholastic, Inc., 1972; 32 pp., $2.95 pb.

——. *Joey.* New York: Prentice-Hall, Inc., 1984; 32 pp., $12.95.

——. *The Once-Upon-A-Time Dragon.* San Diego, Calif.: Harcourt, Brace Jovanovich, Inc., 1982; 32 pp., $11.95.

——. *Round Robin.* New York: Prentice-Hall, Inc., 1982; 32 pp., $11.95.

——. *There's No Such Thing as a Dragon.* New York: Western Publishing, 1975; 24 pp., $1.50 pb.

Kepes, Charles. *Run, Little Monkeys, Run, Run, Run.* New York: Pantheon Books, 1974; 44 pp., $5.99.

Kesselman, Wendy. *Emma.* New York: Doubleday and Co., Inc., 1980; 32 pp., $10.95.

——. *Time for Jody.* New York: Harper & Row, 1975; 40 pp., $5.79.

Kessler, Leonard. *Kick, Pass and Run.* New York: Harper & Row Junior Books, 1966; 64 pp., $10.89.

——. *Mr. Pine's Purple House.* New York: Grosset and Dunlap, 1965; 64 pp., $2.39.

——. *Old Turtle's Winter Games.* New York: Greenwillow, 1983; 56 pp., $8.88.

Kirn, Ann. *The Tale of a Crocodile.* New York: W.W. Norton, 1968; unpaged., $3.95.

Kline, Suzy. *Shhhhh!.* New York: Albert Whitman & Co., 1984; unpaged., $9.25.

Krahn, Fernando. *April Fools.* New York: E.P. Dutton, 1974; 32 pp., $8.95.

Kraus, Robert. *The Little Giant.* New York: Harper & Row, 1967; 32 pp., (no price).

——. *Owliver.* New York: Prentice-Hall Press, 1987; 32 pp., $10.95.

Krauss, Ruth. *The Carrot Seed.* New York: Harper & Row Junior Books, 1945; 24 pp., $10.89.

——. *Eyes, Nose, Fingers, Toes.* New York: Harper & Row, 1964; 32 pp., (no price).

Krisvoy, Juel. *New Games to Play.* Chicago: Follett Publishing Co., 1968; 111 pp., $3.95.

Kroll, Steven. *The Candy Witch.* New York: Holiday House, 1979; 32 pp., $12.95.

——. *One Tough Turkey.* New York: Holiday House, 1982; 32 pp., $12.95.

——. *Pigs in the House.* New York: Parents Magazine Press, 1982; 48 pp., $5.95.

——. *Toot! Toot!.* New York: Holiday House, 1983; 32 pp., $12.95.

LaFontaine, Jean de. *The Hare and the Tortoise.* New York: Golden Press, 1967; 30 pp., $3.95.

Lapp, Carolyn. *The Dentist's Tools.* Minneapolis: Learner Publishing Co., 1961; 31 pp., $2.95.

Lasker, Joe. *Lentil Soup*. New York: Albert Whitman & Co., 1977; 29 pp., $5.75.

Lasson, Robert. *Orange Oliver*. New York: David McKay, 1957; 30 pp., $2.50.

Lenski, Lois. *Debbie Goes to Nursery School*. New York: Henry Z. Walck, 1970; 47 pp., $3.95.

———. *Now It's Fall*. New York: Haney Z. Walck, 1948; 47 pp., $4.95.

———. *Policeman Small*. New York: Henry Z. Walck, 1962; 46 pp., $9.95.

Leonard, Marcia. *Little Owl Leaves the Nest*. New York: Bantam Books, Inc., 1984; 32 pp., $2.75 pb.

Lexau, Joan. *Finders Keepers, Losers Weepers*. Philadelphia: J.B. Lippincott, 1967; 28 pp., $6.50.

———. *Olaf Reads*. New York: Dial Books for the Young, 1965; 53 pp., $6.46.

———. *Who Took the Farmer's Hat?*. New York: Harper & Row, 1963; unpaged., $11.89.

LeSieg, Theo. *I Wish I Had Duck Feet*. New York: Beginner Books, 1965; 64 pp., $6.99.

Littledale, Freya. *The Snow Child*. New York: Scholastic Inc.; 32 pp., $1.95 pb.

Lionni, Leo. *Frederick*. New York: Pantheon Books, 1966; 32 pp., $9.99.

———. *Geraldine, the Music Mouse*. New York: Pantheon Books, 1979; 32 pp., $6.95.

———. *Little Blue and Little Yellow*. New York: Astor-Honor, Inc., 1959; 39 pp., $10.95.

Lobel, Arnold. *Giant John*. New York: Harper & Row Junior Books, 1964; 31 pp., $12.89.

———. *Ming Lo Moves the Mountain*. New York: Greenwillow, 1982; 32 pp., $11.75.

———. *Owl At Home*. New York: Harper & Row Junior Books, 1975; 64 pp., $9.89.

Long, Earlene. *Gone Fishing*. Boston: Houghton Mifflin Co., 1984; 32 pp., $10.95.

Lopshire, Robert. *Put Me in the Zoo*. New York: Beginner Books, 1960; 58 pp., $6.99.

Lucus, Virginia H. and Walter B. Barbe. *Resource Book for the Kindergarten Teacher*. Columbus, Ohio: Zaner-Bloser Inc., 1980; 526 pp., (no price).

Maestro, Betsy. *Big City Port*. New York: MacMillan, 1983; 32 pp., $12.95.

Maestro, Betsy and Giulio Maestro. *Harriet Goes to the Circus*. New York: Crown Publications, Inc., 1977; 30 pp., $12.95.

Maestro, Giulio. *The Remarkable Plant in Apt. 4*. New York: Bradbury Press, 1973; 32 pp., $5.95.

Manning-Sanders, Ruth. *Festivals*. New York: E.P. Dutton, 1973; 169 pp., $8.95.

Manushkin, Fran. *The Adventures of Cap'n O.G. Readamore*. New York: Scholastic, Inc., 1984; 32 pp., $3.95.

Maris, Ron. *Better Move On, Frog!*. New York: Franklin Watts, 1982; 32 pp., $8.90.

Mason, Agnes Leckie and Phyllis Brown Ohania. *God's Wonderful World*. New York: Random House, 1954; 173 pp., $5.59.

Massey, Jeanne. *The Littlest Witch*. New York: Alfred A. Knopf, 1959; unpaged., $3.54.

Mathias, Catherine. *I Can Be a Police Officer*. Chicago: Children's Press, 1984; 32 pp., $7.95.

Matterson, Elizabeth. *Games for the Very Young*. New York: American Heritage Press, 1969; 206 pp., $3.83.

Mayer, Mercer. *Liverwurst Is Missing*. New York: MacMillan, 1981; 32 pp., $10.95.

McCarty, Janet R. and Betty J. Peterson. *Craft Fun: Easy-To-Do Projects with Simple Materials*. New York: Golden Press, 1975; 64 pp., $4.95.

McCloskey, Robert. *Blueberries for Sal*. New York: Viking Penguin, Inc., 1948; 56 pp., $11.95.

McDermott, Gerald. *Anansi the Spider*. New York: Harper & Row Junior Books, 1954; 40 pp., $14.70.

———. *Daniel O'Rourke*. New York: Viking Penguin, Inc., 1986; 32 pp., $11.95.

McGovern, Ann. *Too Much Noise!*. Boston: Houghton Mifflin Co., 1967; 45 pp., $13.95.

McLeod, Emilie. *The Bear's Bicycle*. Boston: Little, Brown & Co., 1975; 32 pp., $12.45.

Meddaugh, Susan. *Maude and Claude Go Abroad*. Boston: Houghton Mifflin Co., 1980; unpaged., $7.95.

Meshover, Leonard and Sally Feistel. *The Monkey That Went to School*. Chicago: Follett Corp., 1978; unpaged., $5.97.

Miller, Donna. *Egg Carton Critters*. New York: Scholastic Books, 1978; 32 pp., $1.95 pb.

Milne, A.A.. *Pooh's Alphabet Book*. New York: E.P. Dutton, 1975; unpaged., $3.27.

Minarik, Else. *Little Bear's Friend*. New York: Harper & Row Junior Books, 1960; 64 pp., $9.89.

Mogensen, Jan. *Teddy Bear and the Chinese Dragon*. Milwaukee, Wis.: Gareth Stevens Inc., 1985; 32 pp., $8.95.

Moncure.. *Wise Owl's Days of the Week*. Chicago: Children's Press, 1981; 32 pp., $10.60.

Moon, Grace. *One Little Indian*. New York: Albert Whitman & Co., 1950; 30 pp., $2.00 pb.

Moss, Jeffrey. *The Sesame Street ABC Storybook*. New York: Random House, 1974; 72 pp., $5.99.

Moss, Jeffrey and David Axelro, Tony Reiss, Bruce Hart, Emily Perl Kingsley and Jon Stone. *The Songs of Sesame Street in Poems and Pictures*. New York: Random House/Children's Television Workshop, 1983; 48 pp., $6.99.

Most, Bernard. *If the Dinosaurs Came Back*. San Diego, Calif.: Harcourt, Brace Jovanovich, Inc., 1978; 32 pp., $11.95.

Muntean, Michaela. *Bicycle Bear*. New York: Parents Magazine Press, 1983; 48 pp., $5.95.

Murphy, Jill. *What Next, Baby Bear!*. New York: Dial Books for the Young, 1984; 32 pp., $10.95.

Myller, Lois. *No! No!*. New York: Simon and Schuster, 1971; 23 pp., $3.07.

Nelson, Esther L.. *Dancing Games for Children of All Ages*. New York: Sterling Publishing Co. Inc., 1973; 72 pp., $16.79.

———. *The Silly Song-book*. New York: Sterling Publishing Co. Inc., 1982; 128 pp., $16.79.

Nichols, Cathy. *Tuxedo Sam: A Penguin of a Different Color*. New York: Random House, 1982; unpaged., $3.95.

Noble, Trinka. *Hansy's Mermaid*. New York: Dial Books for the Young, 1983; 32 pp., $10.89.

———. *Jimmy's Boa Bounces Back*. New York: Dial Books for the Young, 1984; 32 pp., $10.89.

Nolan, Dennis. *Witch Bazooza*. New York: Prentice-Hall, Inc., 1979; 30 pp., $7.95.

Numeroff, Laura. *If You Give a Mouse a Cookie*. New York: Harper & Row Junior Books, 1985; 32 pp., $9.89.

Oppenheim, Joanne. *Mrs. Peloki's Snake*. New York: Dodd, Mead & Co., 1980; 32 pp., $10.95.

———. *Pack-O-Fun.* Spring, 1984. Illinois: Pack-O-Fun Inc.

Palmer, Hap. *Learning Basic Skills Through Music, Vol. 2.* New York: Creative Movement and Rhythmic Exploration.

Palmer, Helen. *I Was Kissed By a Seal at the Zoo.* New York: Random House, 1962; 62 pp., $6.99.

Parish, Peggy. *Let's Celebrate: Holiday Decorations You Can Make.* New York: Greenwillow Books, 1976; 56 pp., $5.95.

———. *Mind Your Manners.* New York: Greenwillow, 1978; 56 pp., $10.88.

Parker, Nancy. *Love From, Aunt Betty.* New York: Dodd, Mead and Co., 1983; 32 pp., $11.95.

Payne, Emma. *Katy No-Pocket.* Boston: Houghton Mifflin Co., 1944; 32 pp., $10.95.

Pearson, Susan. *That's Enough for One Day; J.P.!.* New York: Dial Press, 1977; 26 pp., $5.95.

Peck, Robert. *Hamilton.* Boston: Little, Brown & Co., 1976; 32 pp., $13.45.

Peet, Bill. *The Ant and the Elephant.* Boston: Houghton Mifflin Co., 1972; 48 pp., $11.95.

———. *The Caboose Who Got Loose.* Boston: Houghton Mifflin Co., 1971; 48 pp., $11.95.

Perkins, Al. *Tubby and the Lantern.* New York: Random House, 1971; 64 pp., $3.69.

Perrault, Charles. *Puss in Boots.* Mahwah, N.J.: Troll Associates, 1979; 32 pp., $9.79.

Perry, Margaret. *Rainy Day Music.* New York: M. Evans & Co., Inc., 1970; 160 pp., $5.95.

Petersham, Maud. *The Circus Baby.* New York: MacMillan, 1968; 32 pp., $11.95.

Pflug, Betsy. *Pint Size Fun.* New York: J.B. Lippincott Co., 1972; 38 pp., $3.93.

Piankowski, Jan. *Sizes.* New York: Julian Messner, 1983; 32 pp., $7.97.

Pierce, Jack. *The Freight Train Book.* Minneapolis: Carolrhoda Books, Inc., 1980; unpaged., $9.95.

Pinkwater, Daniel. *The Bear's Picture.* New York: E.P. Dutton, 1984; 39 pp., $10.95.

———. *The Big Orange Splot.* New York: Hastings House Publishers, 1977; 31 pp., $7.95.

———. *I Was a Second Grade Werewolf.* New York: E.P. Dutton, 1983; 32 pp., $9.66.

Pitcher, Caroline. *Cars and Boats.* New York: Franklin Watts, 1983; 30 pp., $8.90.

———. *Games.* New York: Franklin Watts, 1984; 30 pp., $8.90.

Plath, Sylvia. *The Bed Book.* New York: Harper & Row Junior Books, 1976; 40 pp. $11.89.

Polhamus, Jean. *Dinosaur Do's and Don'ts.* Old Tappan, N.J.: Windmill Books, Inc., 1975; 23 pp., $4.95.

Polushkin, Marie. *Mother, Mother I Want Another.* New York: Crown Publications, Inc., 1978; 32 pp., $7.95.

Powell, Harriet. *Games-Songs with Prof. Dogg's Troupe.* London: A & C Black Ltd., 1983; 56 pp., $7.95.

Prelutsky, Jack. *The Terrible Tiger.* New York: MacMillan, 1970; 28 pp., $4.95.

Quackenbush, Robert. *The Holiday Song Book.* New York: Lothrop, Lee and Shepard Co., 1977; 128 pp., $9.20.

———. *The Man on the Flying Trapeze.* New York: J.B. Lippincott Co., 1975; 40 pp., $10.70.

Razzi, James. *Simply Fun! Things to Make and Do.* New York: Parents Magazine Press, 1968; 61 pp., $3.78.

———. *Reaching the Special Learner Through Music.* New York: Silver Burdett Co., 1979; 298 pp., (no price).

Rey, Hans. *Curious George Rides a Bike*. Boston: Houghton Mifflin Co., 1952; 48 pp., $9.95.

Rey, Margaret. *Curious George Flies a Kite*. Boston: Houghton Mifflin Co., 1958; 80 pp., $9.95.

Rockwell, Anne. *Games: (and How to Play Them)*. New York: Thomas Y. Crowell Co., 1973; 44 pp., $10.89.

Rockwell, Harlow. *My Dentist*. New York: Greenwillow, 1975; 32 pp., $11.88.

——. *My Nursery School*. New York: Greenwillow, 1976; 24 pp., $11.75.

Ross, Dave. *Making UFO's*. New York: Franklin Watts, 1980; 32 pp., $7.90.

Ross, Diana. *The Story of the Little Red Engine*. Albuquerque, N.M.: Transatlantic Arts, Inc., nd; 32 pp., $11.95.

Ross, Wilda. *What Did the Dinosaurs Eat?*. New York: Coward, 1972; 47 pp., $3.86.

Rowe, Jeanne. *A Trip Through a School*. New York: Franklin Watts, 1969; 47 pp., (no price).

Sadler, Marilyn. *Alistair in Outer Space*. New York: Prentice-Hall Press, 1984; 48 pp., $12.95.

——. *Alistair's Elephant*. New York: Prentice-Hall Press, 1983; 32 pp., $11.95.

Sauer, Julia. *Mike's House*. New York: Viking Penguin, Inc., 1954; 32 pp., $3.50.

Scarry, Richard. *Richard Scarry's Please and Thank You Book*. New York: Random House, 1978; 29 pp., $4.99.

Scheer, Julian. *Rain Makes Applesauce*. New York: Holiday House, 1964; 36 pp., $12.95.

Schubert, Ingrid. *There's a Crocodile Under My Bed*. New York: McGraw-Hill, 1981; 24 pp., $8.95.

Schweninger, Ann. *The Hunt for Rabbit's Galosh*. New York: Doubleday and Co., Inc., 1976; 30 pp., $4.95.

Scott, Louise Binder. *Rhymes for Learning Times*. Minnesota: T.S. Denison & Co., 1983; 145 pp., $14.95.

Seeger, Ruth Crawford. *American Folk Songs for Children in Home, School, and Nursery School*. New York: Doubleday and Co., Inc., 1948; 193 pp., $6.95.

Seignobosc, Francoise. *Jeanne-Marie Counts Her Sheep*. New York: Charles Scribner's Sons, 1951; 32 pp., $9.95.

Sendak, Maurice. *Really Rosie*. New York: Harper & Row, 1975; 64 pp., $5.95.

Seuss, Dr.. *And to Think I Saw It On Mulberry Street*. New York: Vanguard Press, Inc., 1977; 32 pp., $7.95.

Sharmat, Marjorie. *The Best Valentine in the World*. New York: Holiday House, Inc., 1982; 32 pp., $12,95.

——. *I Don't Care*. New York: MacMillan, 1977; 309 pp., $6.95.

——. *Mitchell Is Moving*. New York: MacMillan, 1985; 47 pp., $3.95.

——. *The Trip*. New York: MacMillan, 1976; 64 pp., $7.95.

Shaw, Charles. *It Looked Like Spilt Milk*. New York: Harper & Row Junior Books, 1947; 28 pp., $11.89.

Sherman, Eileen. *The Odd Potato*. Rockville, Md.: Kar-Ben Copies, Inc., 1984; 32 pp., $10.95.

Short, Mayo. *Andy and the Wild Ducks*. Puente, Calif.: Melmont, 1959; unpaged., (no price).

Shortall, Leonard. *One Way: A Trip With Traffic Signs*. New York: Prentice-Hall, 1975; unpaged., $2.95.

Silverstein, Shel. *The Missing Piece.* New York: Harper & Row Junior Books, 1976; 112 pp., $10.89.

——. *Who Wants a Cheap Rhinoceros?.* New York: MacMillan, 1983; 56 pp., $10.95.

Simon, William L., *The Reader's Digest Children's Songbook.* New York: Reader's Digest Association, Inc., 1985; 252 pp., $24.95.

Globodkin, Louis. *Wide-Awake Owl.* New York: MacMillan, 1958; 28 pp., $2.50.

Slobodkina, Esphyr. *Caps for Sale.* New York: Harper & Row Junior Books, 1947; 48 pp., $10.89.

Snow, Pegeen. *Mrs. Periwinkle's Groceries.* Chicago: Children's Press, 1981; 32 pp., $2.50.

Sommer, Elyse. *Make It With Burlap.* New York: Lothrop, Lee and Shepard Co., 1973; 96 pp., $2.99.

——. *Songs and Rhymes for Little Children.* New York: G & H Publishing Co., 1976; 44 pp., $3.50.

Spier, Peter. *The Star Spangled Banner.* New York: Doubleday and Co., Inc., 1973; 48 pp., $11.95.

Spinelli, Eileen. *Thanksgiving at the Tappleton's.* Reading, Mass.: Addison-Wesley, 1984; 28 pp., $10.70.

Spizman, Robyn Freedman. *Lollipops, Grapes and Clothespin Critters: Quick On-the-Spot Remedies for Restless Children.* Reading, Mass.: Addison-Wesley, 1985; 160 pp., $5.95.

Steig, William. *Sylvester and the Magic Pebble.* Old Tappan, N.J.: Windmill Books, 1969; 30 pp., $4.95 pb.

Stein, Sara Bonnett. *A Hospital Story.* New York: Walker and Co., 1984; 48 pp., $4.95 pb.

Steptoe, John. *The Story of Jumping Mouse.* New York: Lothrop, Lee and Shepard Books, 1984; 40 pp., $11.88.

Stevenson, James. *Could Be Worse!.* Stevenson, James: Greenwillow, 1977; 32 pp., $12.88.

——. *Howard.* Stevenson, James: Greenwillow, 1980; 32 pp., $11.88.

——. *We Can't Sleep.* Stevenson, James: Greenwillow, 1982; 32 pp., $11.88.

——. *Winston, Newton, Elton and Ed.* New York, Greenwillow; 1978; 56 pp., $7.92.

Stolz, Mary. *Emmett's Pig.* New York: Harper & Row Junior Books, 1959; 64 pp., $9.89.

Stone, Benard. *Emergency Mouse.* New York: Prentice-Hall, Inc., 1978; 32 pp., (no price).

Straatviel, Tynne and Carolyn K. Corl. *Easy Art Lessons, K-6.* New York: Parker Publishing Co., Inc., 1971; 154 pp., (no price).

Supraner, Robyn. *Fun With Paper.* Mahwah, N.J.: Troll Associates, 1981; 48 pp., $9.49.

——. *Happy Halloween: Things to Make and Do.* Mahwah, N.J.: Troll Associates, 1981; 48 pp., $9.49.

——. *Rainy Day Surprises You Can Make* : Mahwah, N.J., Troll Associates, 1981; 48 pp., $9.49.

Sur, William and Mary R. Tolbert, William R. Fischer and Adeline McCall. *This is Music, Vol. 2.* Boston: Allyn & Bacon, Inc., 1967; 136 pp., $12.95.

Tafuri, Nancy. *Have You Seen My Duckling?.* New York: Greenwillow, 1984; 24 pp., $10.25.

Tapio, Pat. *The Lady Who Saw the Good Side of Everything.* Boston: Houghton Mifflin Co., 1975; 32 pp., $6.95.

Taylor, Mark. *Henry Explores the Mountains.* New York: Atheneum, 1975; 47 pp., $9.95.

Temklo, Florence. *Felt Craft.* New York: Doubleday and Co., Inc., 1973; 64 pp., $4.96.

Thayer, Catherine. *Gus Was A Friendly Ghost.* New York: William Morrow, 1962; 30 pp., $5.61.

Tietyen, David E. *The Illustrated Disney Song Book.* New York: Random House, 287 pp., $24.95.

Tillstrom. *The Dragon Who Lived Downstairs.* New York: William Morrow, 1984; 48 pp., $11.88.

Titus, Eve. *Anatole and the Piano.* New York: McGraw-Hill, 1966; 32 pp., $6.95.

———. *Anatole Over Paris.* New York: McGraw-Hill, 1961; 32 pp., $6.95.

Tresselt, Alvin. *Rain Drop Splash.* New York: Lothrop, Lee and Shepard Books, 1946; 26 pp., $12.88.

———. *Smallest Elephant in the World.* New York: Alfred A. Knopf, 1959; 27 pp., $2.95 pb.

———. *White Snow, Bright Snow.* New York: Lothrop, Lee and Shepard Books, 1947; 33 pp., $7.25.

Tumpert, Ann. *Nothing Sticks Like a Shadow.* Boston: Houghton Mifflin Co., 1984; 32 pp., $12.95.

Turk, Hanne. *Goodnight Max.* Boston: Neugebauer Press URS, Inc., 1983; 32 pp., $3.50.

Udry, Janice. *Emily's Autumn.* New York: Albert Whitman & Co., 1969; unpaged., (no price).

Upham, Elizabeth. *Little Brown Bear Loses His Clothes.* New York: Putnam Publishing Co., 1978; 24 pp., $2.50.

Van Woerkom, Dorothy. *Harry & Shelburt.* New York: MacMillan, 1977; 48 pp., $6.95.

Vigna, Judith. *Couldn't We Have a Turtle Instead?.* New York: Albert Whitman & Co., 1975; 29 pp., $2.81.

Villarejo, Mary. *The Tiger Hunt.* New York: Alfred A. Knopf, 1959; 28 pp., $2.75.

Vincent, Gabrielle. *Ernest and Celestine.* New York: Greenwillow, 1985; 16 pp., $5.25.

Vinton, Iris. *Folkway's Omnibus of Children's Games.* Harrisburg, Penn.: Stackpole Books Co., 1970; 320 pp., $8.95.

Viorst, Judith. *Try It Again, Sam.* New York: Lothrop, Lee and Shepard Books, 1970; 38 pp., $11.88.

Vogel, Carole. *The Dangers of Strangers.* Minneapolis: Dillon Press, Inc., 1983; 32 pp., $10.95.

Waber, Benard. *But Names Will Never Hurt Me.* Boston: Houghton Mifflin Co., 1976; 32 pp., $13.95.

———. *I Was All Thumbs.* Boston: Houghton Mifflin Co., 1975; 48 pp., $11.95.

———. *Lorenzo.* Boston: Houghton Mifflin Co., 1961; unpaged., $2.70 pb.

Wagner, Jenny. *The Bunyip of Berkeley's Creek.* New York: Bradbury Pres, 1978; 40 pp., $9.95.

Wahl, Jan. *Follow Me Cried Bee.* New York: Crown Publications, Inc., 1976; 29 pp., $5.95.

Watanabe, Shigeo. *I Can Build A House*. New York: Putnam Publishing Group, 1985; 32 pp., $8.95.

Wells, Rosemary. *Max's New Suit*. New York: Dial Books for the Young, 1979; unpaged., $3.50.

Weisgard, Leonard. *The Funny Bunny Factory*. New York: Grosset and Dunlap, 1955; unpaged., (no price).

Weiss, Ellen. *Millicent Maybe*. New York: Avon Books, 1980; 29 pp., $1.50 pb.

——. *Pigs in Space*. New York: Random House, 1983; unpaged., $1.95.

Wessells, Katharine Tyler. *The Golden Song Book*. New York: Golden Press, 1981; 45 pp., $5.95.

Wheeler, Cindy. *Marmalade's Yellow Leaf*. New York: Alfred A. Knopf, 1982; 24 pp., $8.99.

Wildsmith, Brian. *Brian Wildsmith's Fishes*. New York: Franklin Watts, 1968; 30 pp., $5.95.

——. *The Owl and the Woodpecker*. New York: Franklin Watts, 1972; 29 pp., $5.95.

Willard, Nancy. *The Well Mannered Balloon*. San Diego, Calif.: Harcourt, Brace Jovanovich, Inc., 1976; 28 pp., $5.50.

Williams, Barbara. *Albert's Toothache*. New York: E.P. Dutton, 1974; 32 pp., $9.95.

——. *Someday, Said Mitchell*. New York: E.P. Dutton, 1976; 27 pp., $5.95.

Williams, Jay. *Everyone Knows What a Dragon Looks Like*. New York: MacMillan, 1976; 32 pp., $12.95.

——. *The Practical Princess*. New York: Parents Magazine Press, 1969; 40 pp., $8.50.

Willis, Jeanne. *The Tale of Georgie Grub*. New York: Holt, Rinehart & Winston, 1982; 24 pp., $9.95.

Winn, Marie. *The Fireside Book of Children's Songs*. New York: Simon & Schuster, 1966; 223 pp., $12.95.

——. *The Fireside Book of Fun and Games Songs*. New York: Simon & Schuster, 1974; 224 pp., $14.95.

Wirth, Marian Jenks. *Teacher's Handbook of Children's Games*. New York: Parker Publishing Co., 1976; 272 pp., $15.95.

Wolde, Gunilla. *Betsy and the Doctor*. New York: Random House, 1978; 24 pp., $4.99.

——. *Betsy's First Day at Nursery School*. New York: Random House, 1976; 24 pp., $4.99.

Wolf, Benard. *Michael and the Dentist*. New York: Four Winds, 1980; 42 pp., $8.95.

Woolley, Catherine. *The Horse with the Ezster Bonnet*. New York: William Morrow, 1953; 48 pp., $2.00.

——. *Quiet on Account of Dinosaur*. New York: William Morrow, 1964; unpaged., $11.88.

Wright, Dare. *Edith and Little Bear Lend a Hand*. New York: Random House, 1972; 43 pp., $2.95.

Yolen, Jane. *The Emperor and the Kite*. Cleveland, Ohio: William Collins, 1967; 27 pp., $6.99.

——. *The Fireside Songbook of Birds and Beasts*. New York: Simon and Schuster, 1972; 223 pp., $9.95.

——. *No Bath Tonight*. New York: Harper & Row Junior Books, 1978; 31 pp., $11.89.

——. *Rounds and Rounds*. New York: Franklin Watts, 1977; 120 pp., $7.90.

Yorinks, Arthur. *Louis the Fish*. New York: Farrar, Straus and Giroux, Inc., 1980; 32 pp., $10.95.

Yudell, Lynn. *Make a Face.* Boston: Little, Brown & Co., 1970; unpaged., $4.95.

Ziegler, S. *At the Dentist: What Did Chrisopher See?.* Chicago: Chidren's Press, 1976; 32 pp., $4.50.

Zimelman, Nathan. *Positively No Pets Allowed.* New York: E.P. Dutton, 1980; 32 pp., $7.95.

Zindel, Paul. *I Love My Mother.* New York: Harper & Row Junior Books, 1975; 32 pp., $12.89.

Zion, Gene. *Harry By the Sea.* New York: Harper & Row Junior Books, 1965; 28 pp., $11.89.

——. *Harry the Dirty Dog.* New York: Harper & Row Junior Books, 1956; 28 pp., $11.89.

——. *The Plant Sitter.* New York: Harper & Row Junior Books, 1976; 32 pp., $1.95 pb.

——. *Really Spring.* New York: Harper & Row, 1956; 28 pp., $12.89.

——. *The Summer Snowman.* New York: Harper & Row Junior Books, 1955; 30 pp., $12.89.

Zolotow, Charlotte. *I Know an Old Lady.* New York: Greenwillow, 1984; 24 pp., $11.75.

——. *Mr. Rabbit and the Lovely Present.* New York: Harper & Row Junior Books, 1962; 32 pp., $11.89.

——. *The Quarreling Book.* New York: Harper & Row Junior Books, 1963; 32 pp., $9.89.

——. *The Storm Book.* New York: Harper & Row Junior Books, 1952; 28 pp., $12.89.

——. *Summer Is.....* New York: Harper & Row Junior Books, 1972; 32 pp., $10.89.

——. *William's Doll.* New York: Harper & Row Junior Books, 1972; 32 pp., $10.89.

Index to Picture Book Titles

158 INDEX

Index to Authors of
Picture Books

Index to Crafts

Index to Activities

Index to Song Titles